YES,

How to

YOU CAN!

Succeed in Business and Life

ART LINKLETTER

SIMON AND SCHUSTER | NEW YORK

Published by Simon and Schuster
A Division of Gulf & Western Corporation
Simon & Schuster Building
Rockefeller Center
1230 Avenue of the Americas
New York, New York 10020
Designed by Edith Fowler
Manufactured in the United States of America

1 2 3 4 5 6 7 8 9 10

Library of Congress Cataloging in Publication Data

Linkletter, Arthur Gordon, 1912-
   Yes you can!

   1. Success.   I.   Title.
BF637.S8L52   158'.1   79-602
ISBN 0-671-24025-0

Acknowledgment

With deep appreciation I wish to acknowledge the superb, creative editing skills of my friend William Proctor.

To those who want to be better people, or do better at their work, or feel better about life—and are willing to work toward those ends. Yes, you can!

Contents

Introduction

This is a book about how to succeed, and I suppose it's as reasonable for me to write it as for anyone. I began life, literally, with nothing. Given up as an infant by my biological mother, an unmarried young woman from the small town of Moose Jaw in Saskatchewan province in Canada, I was adopted by a poor, middle-aged couple, John and Mary Linkletter.

My adoptive father was one of the warmest men I've ever known, but he had absolutely no ability as a businessman. A part-time evangelical preacher, he also tried selling insurance, running a small general store, and making shoes—all rather unsuccessfully. Eventually, we found ourselves living in a charity home run by a local church in San Diego. Then, Dad Linkletter felt called by God to become a full-time preacher, and we had even less money. And what we did have was usually shared with whatever neighborhood derelict happened to be looking for a meal.

I graduated from high school early and hit the road as a hobo at the tender age of sixteen with the idea of finding my fortune. One of the first things I found, however, was the wrong end of a pistol: My traveling companion and I were held up by a couple of toughs who found us sleeping in a boxcar.

"Put your hands straight out and lie flat!" one of the men ordered. "If this match goes out and I hear anything move, I'll shoot!"

As they searched our pockets and felt around our middles, I wondered if money was all they wanted. I was frightened because I had heard stories of older hobos sexually attacking young boys. Just then, the match went out . . . and was hastily relit. We did not move! The thieves found a dollar and thirty cents on me but missed ten dollars I had sewn into my coat lining. They also took two dollars from my friend, Denver Fox.

The match went out again, and I could tell by their hesitation they were undecided about something. As Denver and I lay there, inches apart in the darkness, I heard the hammer of the pistol click back, and a cold chill ran down my back. I knew they were considering killing us.

There was little risk for them. The rain hammering down on the outside of the boxcar would drown out any noise. Frozen with terror, I thought of my father and how he would have prayed for me, had he known. Suddenly, fear left me, and peace and calm returned. As if in response to my own restored self-assurance, they moved back toward us. Then, I could feel one of the men push something against my arm.

"Here's your thirty cents," he said. "Breakfast money."

During the fourteen months I spent on the road as a vagabond, I worked at a variety of menial jobs, and there was little to indicate that the penniless Art Linkletter would ever amount to much in terms of the world's standard of success. But today I'm a multimillionaire, with income flowing in not only from show business, but from a variety of other sources, including manufacturing, oil and gas, mining, and land development in the United States and Australia. I mention this not to be boastful, but to encourage you to embark on your own road to success by using some simple principles that should speed you along toward your career goals and help you to revise your aspirations upward to new heights of achievement you may not have dreamed possible. As you read these pages, keep in mind where I started. And remember: If I could do it, *you* can too! Yes, you can!

PART ONE

How to Develop Self-Confidence

CHAPTER 1

The Do-What-You-Love-to-Do Principle

Success in life comes to those of us who have confidence in ourselves. If we believe we can do something, and if our faith never wavers as we keep trying to achieve our goals, chances are that we'll succeed. But self-confidence doesn't always come naturally. Most of us have to work hard at building up a sense of assurance about our abilities, just as we have to work at learning a vocational skill or developing strong, healthy family relationships.

The first step toward a better self-image is to take your eyes off others and what they expect of you and to look deep inside yourself. You must become an inner-directed person, rather than one whose life is controlled by the opinions of others. Reacting to social pressure, many people choose the career that offers the fastest route to money, power, fame, or security, rather than the job that would give them the greatest satisfaction. Business prophets constantly say, "This field will offer the highest salaries ten years from now," or "That profession promises the greatest opportunities in the 1980s." And like puppets on a statistical string, everyone heads toward those fields that offer the paths of least resistance.

This approach to life is the biggest mistake anyone can make. In the first place, labor statistics can't give a sure-fire picture of the future. A few years ago, the experts were saying that the outlook was bright for engineers and teachers. Hordes of young people rushed into those fields, only to find that a glut of qualified applicants and some cutbacks in government projects resulted in unemployment instead of a vocational pot of gold. Such disappointments remind me of the 1849 California gold rush, when thousands headed out West, merely to discover that the big claims were already staked out, and their journey had been for nothing.

But even if the statistical Pied Pipers *are* leading you toward certain job opportunities, why get involved in something you may be unhappy doing just because there's an offer of immediate monetary gain? Look at your career with a broader perspective. You have only one life to live, so it makes sense to spend most of your time doing something that will give you the most personal satisfaction.

I learned this lesson the hard way when I was younger. Although I had been a skinny little kid when I graduated from high school, I took a year off to bum around the world, and grew into a six-foot, 185-pounder before I entered college. In fact, I was so big and brawny that the college football coach took one look at me and said, "How about coming out for the football team, Linkletter?"

"I never played football," I replied.

"You never played?" he responded, looking me up and down incredulously.

"No, and I barely made the B-team in basketball in high school—I was just a little guy."

"Well, I think you should try football now. You're certainly big enough," he replied.

So, ready for anything, I showed up when the call went out for those interested in joining the team. But the enthusiasm and self-confidence I'd felt in talking with the coach quickly faded as I listened to the other candidates who crowded around me and discussed their experiences on various high school teams. One guy talked about his pass completion record, and another discussed complicated running plays that I'd never even heard about, much less tried to execute.

With a nervous sweat breaking out on my forehead, I casually got up from my chair and walked to the back of the room. The only way I could make it in this group, I decided, was to wait for everyone else to sign up for a position and put my name down for the job that had the smallest number of candidates.

When the sheet finally reached me, I saw that there was only one guy who had signed up for center, so with a sigh of relief, I put my name down next to his. And for the next few months I spent the most miserable season of my life in athletics.

Center was exactly the wrong kind of position for my abilities and personality. I was a fairly fast runner and an ego-driven, showboat kind of guy. Then, as now, I liked to be seen by people. But I had picked a position where I couldn't run with the ball, so I had no chance to score, and every game I took a constant, painful beating from the opposing line. My head was down in the dirt on every play, and people ran over me from both directions. By the end of the season, I had a veritable path of football cleats up and down my back in *both* directions!

I quit the football team after that year and never played again, but I did go out for basketball and became something of a star. The football coach came back to me after he had watched my basketball performance and said, "You should be an end, Linkletter, or maybe a half-back!" But that initial mistake about which position I should go out for had so tainted my attitude toward the game, that I had no interest in his proposals.

Of course, had I looked inside myself and determined what I really *liked* to do before I picked what looked like the easiest course, my experience as a football player might have been entirely different. I would have realized that doing what I really loved to do would have involved playing in the backfield. The key to self-confidence and also to success and happiness in life is to find out what you really love to do, and then do it!

If you pick those things that you think will make you rich or famous or powerful, you're succumbing to the fallacy of letting the values of society or the approbation of other people control your life. One of the great joys of my life hasn't been counting the millions I've made or seeing how many people recognize me in an airport. Rather, it's knowing that I'm a pro, doing a good job at the work I like best. When I walk out of a television studio and overhear a cameraman say, "Now there goes a guy who knows this business," that's a reward that money can't buy.

To determine your own main interests in life, try this exercise:

Take a pencil and divide a sheet of paper into two columns. Then let your mind soar for a few moments. Imagine yourself at the age of seventy, looking back over your life. As you think back over real and imaginary accomplishments, jot down in the first column those things that you feel would have given you the greatest sense of satisfaction.

Now, still in this mood of fantasy, focus on the present. If you didn't have to worry about money, job security, or any of the other things that tie you down, try to imagine what you would most enjoy doing. You may have devoted your life to accounting, banking, real estate, teaching, or secretarial work, but is that what you would *really* like to do if you had a choice? Write down the work or pastimes that appeal to you most in the second column on your paper.

After you've finished with this exercise, lean back in your chair and compare your two lists. Then compare them to what you're actually doing. Chances are there will be some similarities on your lists, but they'll probably be quite different from what you're really doing.

In my travels and conversations with people from all over, I've discovered that a large majority are working at jobs that they find personally unrewarding. And even if they like their jobs, they'd prefer to do something else if they didn't have to worry about money.

Some people I know let their jobs choose them, rather than choosing their jobs. Many were guided into their present work by a parent or other authoritative figure. Still others took summer jobs while in college or graduate school and moved into the same occupations on a full-time basis because there were immediate openings available on graduation. Some took what they considered temporary jobs, but along came marriage and children, and making a change became more and more difficult.

A basic principle of career development is that the longer you wait to change jobs, the harder it gets because you stand to lose more in terms of seniority and fringe benefits. Also, the longer you're in a particular job, the more familiar it becomes, and the familiar is preferable to the unknown. Things may not be so good where you are, but at least your gripes and dissatisfactions are familiar. The unknown, on the other hand, always presents a risk. It may offer more opportunities in the long run, but it may also create worse problems. So rather than strike out on an uncertain career adventure, you prefer to hang on to the mediocre experience you know so well.

I'm not advocating a hedonistic, do-your-own-thing-to-the-exclusion-of-others philosophy. Far from it. I'm a great believer in the importance of concentrating on the needs of others, developing strong family ties, and being dependable in your human relationships. But I also feel that if you get involved in those things that you enjoy most, you'll find the quality of your relationships with others improving. If you have a confident, positive attitude about yourself, your friends and loved ones will respect you and enjoy your company more.

Finally, if you like your work, you will put in more time trying to achieve your goals. There's a built-in endurance that energizes you when you're interested in a project. I've always found that when I get involved in activities I love, it's nearly impossible for me to tackle those tasks in a half-hearted way. At this stage in my life, for example, I could easily just quit working altogether and retire, spending all my time with my family in travel and at our estate in Bel Air. But instead, I speak ninety to one hundred times a year all over the world at conventions, church meetings, colleges, and positive-thinking rallies because that's what I love to do.

Think back to the last book you really enjoyed. Remember how you didn't want to put it down—didn't even want to go to sleep until you finished that next chapter? Your daily tasks can be just as compelling as a page-turning thriller if you choose them with care, in light of your real interests.

"But what about money?" you may ask. "I'm an assistant sales manager, but what I like most is working weekends as a carpenter in my basement, making furniture. You're not seriously suggesting that I quit my job and start building chairs, are you?"

I'm not necessarily recommending that you drop your present, lucrative job and hop into a business that pays a quarter as much when you have kids you're trying to get through college—though there are some people who do just that. I read the other day about a man who left a high-paying advertising position to open a grocery store in Vermont, and he was quoted, "You wouldn't get me back on Madison Avenue for $200,000 a year!"

But what I am suggesting is this: If you dislike your present job or are in a field that holds little fascination for you except for the money or the promise of prestige, consider furniture making or some other all-consuming interest as an avocation while you think about your long-term goals in life.

If you're doing what you love to do, you'll not only spend more time at your job, but you'll also do better quality work. People will admire your efforts, and their approval will reinforce your own enjoyment. You'll bound out of bed in the morning actually looking forward to your tasks. And inevitably, the monetary rewards will come. In most cases, the law of supply and demand dictates that the better job you do, the better you'll get paid. And the more your business grows, the more people you'll have working for you and the more your power will increase. Finally, as you do fine work in your furniture shop, the public and consumer advocates will shower acclaim on you as the last of a dying breed of fine craftsmen. So there you have it—money, power, and fame could all be within your grasp from the moment you leave the corporate job you hate and strike off on the furniture building business you love.

This progression from doing what you like, to self-confidence, happiness, and success, is a very real possibility for you or anyone else, with one very important limitation: You have to be realistic about your abilities. You may think you would love to be a professional basketball player, but if you're forty and five-feet-two, your chances of achieving this ambition are nil. That's why it's important not only to affirm the do-what-you-love-to-do principle, but also to take an inner strength test to determine realistically what life goals you have the best chance of accomplishing.

CHAPTER 2

Your Inner Strength Test

It's a basic failing of human nature that we tend to emphasize our weaknesses rather than our strengths. And one of the main reasons is that the reinforcements we get from the people around us are negative rather than positive.

Most of your friends and loved ones accept your good behavior without comment. But when you do something wrong, boy, do you catch it! If you do a job well, your boss just grunts or nods or ignores you. At most, he favors you with "Joe, that was a pretty good job." But if you make a mistake, you're likely to be hit with all the gory specifics of your poor performance: "Do you realize you have the memory of a duck? Can't you ever get anything right? Now look at all the errors you made on this report. . . ."

Too often, stress on the negative characterizes personal associations, including family relationships. For example, few of us are consistently, consciously thankful for kids who make it through high school and college without getting into trouble with the law or with drugs. Very few practice "preventive family love" by analyzing and improving on what they're doing *right* in encounters with children and loved ones.

When was the last time you asked yourself: "I wonder why my daughter hasn't tried marijuana? What influences are keeping her away from drugs, and how can I reinforce those influences?"

But if she *does* get involved with marijuana or hard drugs, you're quite likely to chastise yourself after the fact: "Why didn't I notice her eyes were dilated, her grades were slipping, and her circle of friends had changed? Why didn't I insist she get home at a decent hour?"

I can't count how many parents I've met who are wallowing in such might-have-beens and self-recriminations over kids they have lost to drugs. I often tell them, "Stop it! You're whipping yourself for something you can't change now." And I can speak to them with some authority because I lost a daughter to drugs, as I'll discuss in some depth later in this book. But they're so conditioned to focus on the negative—on their failings—that it's difficult, if not impossible, for them to discern their strong points and utilize them more effectively.

Because you can't rely on other people to reinforce your strengths—or even to tell you what they are—it's essential to your own self-confidence that you do some soul-searching right now to determine your natural abilities and talents. Then you can begin to build a successful life around these strong points.

When I was a youngster, just out of high school, I needed odd jobs for the year I spent bumming around before I entered college. But I had very few skills to commend me. Although I occasionally applied for jobs as a secretary, I couldn't take dictation and knew nothing about filing. There was one thing I *could* do, however, and that was to type faster than anyone else at San Diego High School. I had won a prize for speed typing, and I always stressed that skill when I went out looking for a secretarial job.

"Mr. Smith," I'd say, "I want that secretarial job you're offering, and there's one thing I want to tell you at the outset. I was a champion typist in San Diego, and I'd like to give you a demonstration of what I can do if you can spare a moment."

Then I'd take a piece of paper, whirl it into a typewriter, and give him a demonstration of speed typing that would leave his head spinning. By the time I had finished, he would be so enthralled by my skill he would have forgotten about whether I could take shorthand or whether I had even held another job before.

Your strongest point may be something so familiar to you that it may not even seem important. But if you sit down and try to think how many other people have this talent, you may find you're unique. I know one man who worked his way up to become the senior vice-president in a good-sized corporation. As far as I could tell, he had none of the ordinary executive strengths to commend him. There was nothing outstanding about his education, his intelligence, or his ability as a manager. But after pondering what I knew about him, I realized he could do two things better than almost anyone else. First of all, he played a fine game of tennis and was constantly in demand as a partner by the high-level executives in his company. And secondly, he was one of the best story-tellers I've ever met.

He would walk into important business meetings with a string of jokes about labor relations, management problems, financial issues, and almost any other topic that might arise. When one of these issues had been discussed seriously for a time, this fellow, with just the right joke, would break the tension or even inject a new perspective on the issue. His colleagues then came away from the meeting saying, "This guy really makes a point with his witticisms. And he's so pleasant to be around." Sufficiently aware of the importance of his talent, he spent as much time reading through materials to get funny stories and jokes as he did in hard research on matters more directly related to the business.

Another kind of strength that I noticed at meetings with writers on the "People Are Funny" show was what John Guedel, my partner, and I used to call the "heart of the artichoke" talent. An occasional person we'd work with would have that rare ability to listen to the jumble of ideas and observations during our half-hour discussions and then be able to jot down the essence of what had been said. While everyone else was fiddling with the artichoke leaves of the discussion, he would push all the nonessentials aside and go right to the heart of the matter.

Now, that kind of ability may seem insignificant in career planning, but a heart-of-the-artichoke person is invaluable in getting a discussion back on the right track and saving valuable time for everyone involved. Any perceptive, high-level executive will value that ability if he's made aware of it, and if that's your talent, it's up to you to dust off this pearl you possess and show it off.

To help you ferret out your own strengths, as well as to put your weaknesses into perspective, try this inner strength test. First of all, take five full minutes and write down what you consider your strongest points. Remember as you're writing that seemingly insignificant things, like an incisive sense of humor and an ability to sum up an argument, may be the very thing that can carry you to the heights of accomplishment and success. Then, when you've finished with your strengths, list your weaknesses.

Now go back to your strength list and jot down any you have remembered while writing down your weaknesses. Finally, compare the two lists. If you have listed more strengths than weaknesses, you tend to be a self-assured, confident person who realizes his potential for success. But if you included more weak points, you are probably a person who doesn't really understand his full potential.

The person who focuses on his strengths is the person who makes the best use of his talents and moves ahead in the world. This positive thinker is also the most likely to find the challenges of life exciting, rather than overwhelming, and more often than not, he discovers happiness.

If your list of weaknesses is longer, it's not because you *actually* have more weak than strong points. It's because you *think* your flaws outweigh your talents. Perhaps you detailed your weaknesses more than your strengths. For example, you may have written, "I get along pretty well with people," under your strengths, but under weaknesses, "In doing reports at work, I'm a slow reader, a mediocre writer, only so-so in organizing my research time, not fast enough in comprehending new subject matter. . . ." In other words, you've gone into minute detail on your problems with writing reports, but in the all-important area of personal relations—where you feel you are strong —you spoke only in the vaguest generalities. As a result, you have painted a false, negative picture of yourself on your strength–weakness scale. If you've slipped into this pattern of reinforcing your negative rather than your positive points, spend some time reworking your lists to give a truer picture of yourself.

Even after you've gained confidence upon determining what your precise strengths are, you still face the challenge of selling those strengths to other people. As a younger man, I learned it was always essential to face my shortcomings squarely, but then to push them out of my mind and concentrate on the positive things I had to offer to prospective employers. When I was being considered for various radio jobs years ago, for example, I thought, I know this guy can hire a more famous person than I am. And he can find somebody who's better looking. But I know how to do interviews well, and for this particular job, I think I can do a better job than anyone else under the circumstances.

I also tried to tell prospective employers about my strengths through explanatory anecdotes rather than in a direct, abrasive way, and I've known successful salesmen who have taken the same approach. A salesman of manufacturing equipment, for example, might get a door slammed in his face by saying to a potential buyer, "Your production system is all wrong, and I can show you a much better way to do things."

A more effective way to present his strength, which involves the new machinery he's selling, might go like this, "I've been selling in this field for ten years, Mr. Jones, and I think you'd be interested in a recent experience I had with another client who actually doubled his production!"

Few prospective buyers would refuse to listen after

such an enticing opening, so the salesman continues: "When I first walked into that man's plant, he said, 'We don't have any use for your equipment because it cuts our steel the wrong way.' But I told him, 'Look, suppose I told you if you started cutting your steel this new way, you could do everything you've been doing and in addition, use the scraps of steel you're throwing away to start an entirely new business.' Well, that buyer was interested enough to buy $80,000 worth of our new equipment. And he's embarked on an entirely new business that has increased his earnings by 50 percent."

This salesman has illustrated that he's experienced in the field (selling for ten years), he's innovative (new equipment), and most important, he can increase a client's business. He puts his strengths on display in a nonboastful, compelling framework that's designed to increase his chances of business success and also to enhance and reinforce a healthy view of his own abilities.

But following the do-what-you-love-to-do principle and passing the inner strength test can advance you only just so far on the road to self-confidence and success. It's also important to have an overall plan for your life, and that's where intelligent goal-setting comes into play.

CHAPTER 3

Goal-Setting:
The Roadmap to Success

Every successful person I've ever known has had a definite set of goals he was shooting for—a specific dream to turn into reality. But the way those goals are defined can mean the difference between success and failure in life.

Before you start drawing up a blueprint for your future, consider these four principles, which I've found helpful in arriving at my own life's goals:

1. SUCCESS ITSELF IS A JOURNEY, NOT A DESTINATION. Your goals for success, therefore, should not be final destinations, but only way stations on your journey through life.

2. MAKE YOUR PERSONAL GOALS SPECIFIC, BUT DON'T SET THEM IN CONCRETE. No matter how carefully you plan things, you must be prepared for the unexpected, the divine surprise which no man can predict but every successful man must learn to accommodate.

3. TRUE SUCCESS ALWAYS RESULTS IN SOME MEASURE OF HAPPINESS. There's something fundamentally wrong with an achievement that doesn't leave you reasonably satisfied and happy.

4. REACHING A GOAL SHOULD ALWAYS MAKE YOU A BETTER PERSON. Always try to make doing a better job

your primary motivation at any given moment. I'm frequently asked, "At your age, Art, what do you want to do?"

I want to do better. I want to talk better, write better, be a better person and friend. I have no desire to accumulate a specific quantity of money or to make the list of the ten richest people in Hollywood. Nor do I find acquiring large quantities of anything else to be wholly satisfying. What gives me the greatest sense of well-being is to be confronted by an exciting job opportunity—one that surprises me—and then to work hard and see the quality of my performance improve.

I do believe in setting definite goals, but I've learned that success is never a straight trip, from one point to another, and may involve a more circuitous route than first expected. Have an idea about where you're going and what goal you want to achieve; otherwise, it's doubtful that you'll ever get there. At the same time, remain flexible about the exact path you take as you move toward the major destinations of your life. Inevitably, when you incorporate this flexibility in your planning, life becomes a much richer experience, and the goals you originally set for yourself turn out to be only a pale shadow of what you can really achieve.

When I was a youngster, I became fascinated with the Chautauqua circuit—those traveling lectures and concerts that educated and entertained the public in the late nineteenth and early twentieth centuries before the advent of radio and television. In fact, I decided that what I really wanted to become was one of those speakers, especially after I heard Elwood P. Bailey, one of the greatest lecturers to come to San Diego. Bailey was to speaking what Al Jolson was to singing. Nothing was pale gray; everything was Olympian, broad, grandiose. His rolling, sonorous tones and flowery figures of speech absolutely captivated me. He became my hero. On many afternoons after the workmen had gone home, I would walk over to the unfinished Woodrow Wilson Junior High School auditorium, climb up on the stage, and speak—imitating Bailey's style—to the rows of unfinished seats.

One of my greatest frustrations when I reached college age was realizing that the day of the Chautauqua circuit had passed. I figured I was living in the wrong era and sadly began to cast about for another career. But the idea of speaking to others, influencing them through my verbal skills, stuck with me, and that may be one of the reasons I settled on teaching as an occupation. My starting salary would be $120 a month, which seemed pretty good to me. If I really put my nose to it, I thought, I might get up to $300 a month before I retire, and who would need more money than that?

But though my goal remained speaking to others, the exact form it would take wasn't something I could anticipate as I tried to plot my career in college. Unexpectedly, I was offered a job working at a local radio station at the stunning figure of $125 a month, $5 more than the school-teaching job would have paid. A difference of only $5 a month doesn't seem like enough money to cause me to change my career goals, but sometimes a trifle can tilt the scales dramatically. I accepted the offer, and my career goals immediately became more ambitious. Now, instead of that $300-a-month ceiling, I realized I might someday make $1000 or more a month as a network radio announcer. My ultimate goal of speaking to people, influencing them through my oral presentations, remained the same, but the path to that goal had changed dramatically. And it has continued to change, through my television shows (which I *never* could have anticipated, even in my wildest fantasies, as I embarked on my radio career) to my present speaking dates to audiences of thousands around the country.

In a way, my career has come full circle, and I'm now doing what I originally set out to do as a youngster. I've created my own Chautauqua circuit as I deliver addresses at colleges, town halls, conventions, and positive-thinking rallies. And because I now have a wealth of varied experience to draw upon, I know I'm a much better lecturer than I might ever have been, had I been able to embark on that calling fresh out of college.

Success, then, doesn't involve formulating a certain goal and marching forward, over a well-defined, predetermined path, to seize the prize. Life is too complicated and unpredictable. Instead, success means reaching a succession of plateaus throughout life. You may know what your ultimate goal is all along, but more likely, you'll find yourself constantly expanding and changing your plans as you move from one plateau to another. Most of you make some progress in one phase of your career; then you seem to stand still for a while. But what you're actually doing is regrouping your intellectual and creative powers to prepare for the next surge forward, to a still higher and more demanding plateau of success. When you reach these new heights, you look back on the previous level of achievement and say, "Hey, how could I ever have been satisfied back there," even though at the time, that former plane of success may have appeared to be your ultimate accomplishment in life.

I remember how much fun I had interviewing kids on

the CBS "House Party" shows on radio and television. During the twenty-five years I did those programs, I rode a high crest of popularity and wrote a best-selling book, *Kids Say the Darndest Things*, which was based on that series. Subsequently, I plunged into a number of challenging business ventures: oil exploration, real estate, manufacturing, and other enterprises that challenged my management abilities. And I also wrestled with knotty issues like drug abuse and positive thinking on the lecture platforms as often as one hundred times a year.

When I recently accepted an offer to try a pilot for another television show interviewing children, therefore, I was a different person from the fellow who had moved up from a radio announcer's post back in the 1930s. As I did the pilot, I had some marvelous interviews with some of the brightest kids I've ever encountered, but somehow I didn't get the same psychic "kick" I once had. There were still plenty of cute, unexpected answers from them, like the five-year-old boy who readily acknowledged he was one of the brightest kids in his class.

"Do you know who the president of the United States is?" I asked him.

"Oh, yes, George Washington," he replied, perfectly serious.

"What does he look like?" I asked.

"I never saw his face, but it's red, white, and blue," the boy responded.

"Did you ever hear the name Jimmy Carter?"

"Oh, yes, I heard that; he's a movie star."

Now, this is lovely, funny stuff, and I laugh at it myself. But I don't get the same feeling of accomplishment I once did. Spending all my time now doing what I did

in the 1950s and '60s would be like living on a steady
diet of meringue, and after having plenty of meat and
potatoes during the past decade, I can't be satisfied with
meringue anymore. I still concentrate on entertaining
people in parts of my speeches, but no matter how much
fun I have, I always try to leave my audiences with
something of substance, some message or purpose. My
specific goals in life—in other words, my yardsticks for
personal success—have evolved as I've moved from one
plateau to the next.

When you're young, one of the most difficult things to
understand is that material possessions are not the cru-
cial elements in a successful life. At one time or another
you've said to yourself, I'm going to be successful
when I have X dollars in the bank, or when I can buy a
house in Grosse Pointe, or when people all over the country know who I am. But I guarantee you that acquiring
these things doesn't give you a sense of lasting accomplishment. When you make that first million, it's not
what you thought it would be. And the fact that most
people can recognize you on the street doesn't insure
your happiness. There's nothing wrong with reaching out
for goals like money and fame, but when they become the
all-consuming interest in your life, you're likely to find
yourself moving farther and farther away from that much
worthier and more satisfying ambition—becoming a better person.

Now I'd like you to take a few minutes and jot down
some of the most important things you'll ever put on
paper. Think for a moment about where you're heading
in life. What do you want to achieve in ten years, five
years, or before the end of this year? Refer back to the

exercises in which you decided what you'd most like to do, and the strengths and weaknesses that might help or hinder you. Now the time has come to settle on a definite game plan for your life. You know that you'll probably change these goals as you get older. Your horizons will expand and shift as you move from one plateau to another. But it's essential that you set some targets and get moving toward them. Otherwise, you'll have no choice at all in the direction that your life takes.

First of all, decide what your long-term goals should be. Think in terms of five to ten years from now. Any longer period becomes more wishful thinking than realistic planning. Next, settle on some intermediate goals, something you'd like to accomplish by this time next year. Most of these intermediate goals should be tied in to the longer-term goals you've set for yourself. Finally, outline a plan of action on a short-term basis—for this next month and even the upcoming week. Again, your immediate goals should move you a step or two toward achieving the intermediate and long-term objectives. And getting started right away on your life plan will encourage you to take your goal-setting seriously and avoid procrastination.

You've taken some positive steps in this chapter by setting some realistic goals for yourself, and I am confident that you'll not only achieve many of those goals but will go far beyond them. At the same time, since life never offers a straight path from the achievement of one ambition to the next, you must follow new, unexplored roads if you hope to succeed in business and life.

There will be times when everything seems to be going against you, and in those periods, it's easy to fall into a negative frame of mind or even be tempted to give up.

These setbacks have come close to shattering me, too, but there are ways of making the negative side of life work for you. To understand how this process works, I want to introduce you now to what I call the negative basis of positive thinking.

PART TWO

The Negative Basis
of Positive Thinking

CHAPTER 4

It's All Right for Things to Go Wrong

Although we are all imperfect creatures, for some reason we expect to be perfect. We give lip service to the fact that we're fallible, but when mistakes occur, we inevitably castigate ourselves for being such terrible failures.

I always chuckle when I watch a tennis pro playing a near-perfect match on television and then see him make an amateurish error or hear a linesman make a bad call against him. I can almost always predict what will happen next with most players: They start to brood about their misfortune, and their whole game falls apart.

I'm exactly like that myself sometimes. Things will go wonderfully for me, and I'll begin to think I'm entitled to uninterrupted happiness, until some little thing happens to remind me that I live in the real world, with accidents, mistakes, and failures. In those moments, I think of the man who walked out of his home one day and saw a stranger standing on a nearby corner.

"Here's $100 for you," the stranger said, and the businessman nearly fell on his face with surprise and happiness. It was a great event in his life—perhaps the best thing that had ever happened to him that early in the morning.

The next day, he walked out of his house and found the same guy there, and once again, the stranger slapped $100 into the businessman's palm. Again, he was ecstatic!

The same Good Samaritan was there on the same corner, day after day for several months with the cash gifts, and soon the businessman expected him to be there. He took the generosity for granted, until one day, the stranger failed to show up.

"Where is that guy?" the businessman complained, resentfully. "What's the matter with him? Where's my $100?"

Like this ungrateful character, you so often accept your *good* luck without thinking and dwell on the *bad* things that happen and blow them out of proportion. When you think about it, most people have far more good luck than bad, far more happiness than sadness. Most people are healthy, for example, yet when they experience serious sickness for the first time, it dominates their thinking and may turn them into basically negative personalities. If you have to go into the hospital for an operation, you may find yourself flat on your back for a time with tubes up your nose. Or if you break a leg, you will find yourself on crutches and in a cast for a couple of months. During those times of ill health and immobility, you come to appreciate how great it is to have control over your body and to be free of physical pain and discomfort. Just discharged from the hospital, you revel in your good health, now that your illness has passed. But in a few days, with the doctor's bills in your hands, it's a different story. Your health is back, but something else that's negative has entered your life again, to dominate your thinking and your relationships with others.

The first step in putting this negativism in proper perspective is to confront the unpleasant side of life squarely and accept it as a fact of life. I'm somewhat different from most positive thinkers in this regard, because I believe that the only valid basis for positive thinking is to assume that bad things are going to happen to you from time to time. If you take the attitude that things aren't always going to be peaches and cream, you'll be especially happy and thankful when they do go well, and you'll avoid dismay when they don't go as you had hoped.

This approach to life will help you to become a realist, not a pessimist, and you'll be better prepared to capitalize on negative events. In my own case, for example, I used to expect people to walk up to me on the street and say nice things, but somehow compliments would occasionally get twisted into devastating criticisms of my looks, my age, and even my performing ability.

One time I pumped myself up emotionally for a positive-thinking speech in my hotel room and then burst out of the door on a wave of high-flown, happy thoughts. But before I reached the elevator, a little old lady rushed up to me, grabbed my sleeve, and said, "Mr. Linkletter, I'm proud to say I'm one of your oldest fans!"

"Well, isn't that nice," I replied.

"Yes," she said, "I've watched your career from the beginning to the very end of it."

On other occasions, I've been confronted with comments like these:

"You look just exactly like the late Art Linkletter." Or, "You look better alive than you do on TV!"

I suppose it would be easy to get upset by such remarks, and if I took them seriously, I probably wouldn't be able to get out of bed in the morning. But actually, by conditioning myself to expect them, I've come to recognize these comments as some of the funniest lines I've heard. And I frequently use them in my speeches.

Such experiences have convinced me that fine-tuning your sense of humor—learning to laugh at yourself and at unpleasant situations that confront you—is one of the best techniques for turning a negative incident into something more positive. Also, the more you can stand back and smile at what's happening to you, the cooler your head will be, and the more resilient and effective you'll become in dealing with tough, embarrassing challenges.

I'm reminded of an experience I had one recent winter in Appleton, Wisconsin. A Lutheran society had brought me there to speak on drug abuse to various civic groups, and one of the audiences on the schedule had been listed as a group of local students.

"How long do you want me to talk to these students?" I asked the coordinator.

"About an hour," he replied.

"That's fine, because I just love to talk to young people," I said, assuming the kids would be high school age.

But when I walked onto the stage, I found I was standing in front of several hundred second-graders, and the auditorium wasn't an auditorium at all, but a gym, with mats spread on the floor for my little listeners. Not only that, they had been waiting for me to arrive for two hours, without even one coloring book to keep them occupied. They were wriggling and squirming and kicking and scratching and doing everything else a child will do when he's at his wits' end. It suddenly struck me that this was the first time I had ever actually looked into a huge barrel of worms.

Standing in front of them, with only a few seconds before they got quiet, I silently had to revise all my figures of speech, my jokes, even the way my speech was organized. But I knew the positive can always come from the negative if you're in the right frame of mind, with sense of humor intact. Sure enough, as I stood there waiting calmly and laughing to myself at the absurdity of the situation, a miraculous lightning bolt of inspiration struck me.

"Hello there, boys and girls," I said. "I've come all the way from Hollywood to tell you about the most exciting picnic you've ever been on in your life. This is going to be an adventure in the woods, with all kinds of animals and mountain peaks and strange-looking bugs."

They were already following me intently, and I was interested myself to see exactly where my story was going to go. "We're on that picnic right now, because life, for each of you, is a picnic. From the time you're born until the time you die, you're on an exciting trip through unknown country. Some of the birds you see are familiar and some are strange, and there are all kinds of unexpected sights: babbling brooks and treehouses and meadows where you can play Hide and Seek or King of the Mountain. How many of you have ever been on a picnic?" I asked, and many hands went up. They were participating with me now, recalling or fantasizing how much fun they had had with their parents and friends.

"But you know, even though picnics are a lot of fun, when you're out there in the woods, there are a few things you shouldn't do. You can't step into a river without knowing how deep it is, or you might drown. And you can't just walk up to any animal, because it might bite you. If you see a big bear, you're going to be sensible enough to duck behind a tree. Some of the plants may be poison oak and ivy, so you have to stay away from those.

"Well, just as you have to be careful on a picnic so that you won't spoil your fun, you also have to be careful about certain special things in life. For example, a match is good because it helps you light the stove so you can cook food and eat; but it can be bad because if you're careless with it, you might burn the house down. And knives are important as tools, but they can also cut and injure you. There's something else called drugs, which are good when you're sick, but drugs can be very bad if used for the wrong reasons or in the wrong amounts. . . ."

By the time I had finished, the kids were entranced, and I know my message got across to many of them because of the volume of mail I received after I returned to California. Some of the praise, as usual, was faint, but I appreciated it just the same. One little boy wrote: "Mr. Linklettuce, you are the best speaker I've ever heard. P.S., you're the only speaker I've ever heard." Another little girl said, "Thank you for coming to our school and leading us into drug abuse."

As a result of this experience, I'm sure I'd feel more comfortable confronting a similar challenge in the future. Every problem can be an opportunity if you just shake off your tendency to think negatively and try to find the lesson the troublesome situation can teach you. Take a recent television disaster I faced. I spent a great deal of time putting together a pilot for ABC involving brief interviews with kids that would be shown as a feature on one of the talk shows. Dozens of children were brought in, and with the cameras rolling, I talked to them until I was nearly hoarse, and got some of the best responses I'd ever had with that sort of format. Then, just as I had finished and was packing up to go home, I got the bad news: One of the key cameras hadn't been working properly. Some of my best footage had been lost entirely or recorded only partially.

I know one nationally known comedian who would have set the studio on fire at such news. Still, it was a terrible blow, and I was naturally upset and depressed when they told me. But I didn't swear or berate anyone. I didn't chew people up and spit them out—and that's almost standard practice in the industry when a stupid mistake like this occurs. I'm not trying to give the impression I'm a better person than anyone else. On the contrary, my reactions were almost purely pragmatic in that I knew, from experience, that it wouldn't do me or anyone else any good to blow my stack. The *Book of Proverbs* says that as a man "thinketh in his heart, so is he" (Proverbs 23:7), and I know after letting my emotions get the best of me on other occasions, that hostile, vengeful thinking feeds on itself and eventually destroys your effectiveness unless you immediately put your frustrations and failures behind you and get started on correcting your mistakes.

So I wallowed in my pain silently for a few moments, but a few moments only. Or as Dryden wrote, "I'm a little wounded, but I am not slain; I will lay me down to bleed a while, Then I'll rise and fight with you again." Before I left the studio, I called the staff together and said: "This is a terrible blow, but let's organize tomorrow and see if there's anything we can salvage. We won't let this get us down; we'll just do a better show next time. We'll eliminate the kids who didn't turn out well and just look on today as a huge dress rehearsal."

That's the only attitude that makes any sense to me, and I only wish I could always follow my own advice.

Whenever I fall back into self-pity or excessive rage at something that's gone wrong, I try to repeat some advice I heard from John Wooden, the great U.C.L.A. basketball coach. He said, "Things turn out best for the people who make the best of the way things turn out," and that's become my philosophy too. When things outside your control intervene to disrupt your day, you're certainly entitled to a certain amount of emotional disturbance. No one is a robot, and I believe it's good for your emotional health to let out some of the anger and frustration you feel. But don't allow yourself to continue foaming at the mouth or cursing God. Find a proverb or a line of poetic wisdom that you can make your slogan and call to mind when the going gets rough. I got a letter from Charles Colson the other day, for example, and he jotted down "Romans 8:28" below his signature. That verse reads, "And we know that all things work together for good to them that love God, to them who are the called according to his purpose." What could be more positive than to dwell on something like that, rather than to brood about a disaster that's already happened?

But even if you manage to get over that first wave of anger, there's still a residue of worry and regret that often remains for long periods after a personal failure or misfortune. Sometimes it's not possible to eliminate that feeling of anxiety or depression immediately, but there are ways you can put your worry to work for you.

CHAPTER 5

Put Worry to Work for You

Worries and anxieties are our primary stumbling blocks to a joyful, effective life. Concern about little things—whether we said the wrong thing at a dinner party last night—may nag at our minds for hours and destroy an entire day's concentration. Big disasters and tragedies—or just the *possibility* of such tragedy—may taint our emotions for days, weeks, or longer.

Nobody is immune to these worries, of course, but there are a number of ways to control them and actually put them to work to create a positive out of a negative experience. When a worry enters your life, the basic idea is not to say: "Oh, no, that happiness I was feeling was just too good to last. Now it's back to my usual state of being upset and bothered." Rather, your attitude should be: "Okay, now for a little excitement in life! The lull is over and the adventure and challenge are about to begin!"

In other words, try to accept worry, disruption, and uncertainty as positive forces that can be harnessed and put to work for you, rather than as unmitigated disasters and setbacks. Here are a few guidelines I've found helpful in putting worry to work:

1. WHEN WORRY SETS IN, ACTION SHOULD BEGIN. At the first sign of a problem, I immediately marshal my inner strength and prepare to turn the bad situation to my favor. When I first began to experience some financial success in show business, I started looking around for investment opportunities, and one of the first things that appealed to me and a few other young, up-and-coming entertainers was an oil well drilling deal near Tulsa, Oklahoma. It soon became apparent, though, that we had made a bad investment. Or, as I like to tell it, we hit liquid on our very first well at 3500 feet, but it turned out to be ketchup from an old hamburger stand that was buried in an Oklahoma dust storm.

Now, I got worried at the outset when I saw my hard-earned money being poured into several hopelessly dry wells. But instead of sinking into a quagmire of anxiety, I sat down and evaluated what I was learning from the experience. In the first place, I decided that oil drilling was too risky to be done with any money other than discretionary, extra funds. But in evaluating my finances again, I saw that I did have some extra money, so I wouldn't automatically rule out further investments in oil and gas. The question that faced me was, What's the best way to approach this kind of investment?

And that led me to my second insight. I saw that drilling in deals with wildcatters who were operating on a "wing and a prayer," rather than sound research, was not the way to do it. So I began to study the field. Then, in a few months, I got back into the oil business again, but this time I bought smaller pieces of deals with more basic value lying near proven oil and gas production. I looked for firms that employed scientific seismic data and cut the risks for investors in other ways. Investing in such "plays" cost me more for comparable percentages of ownership, but I no longer felt I was engaging in a crap shoot on some unexplored prairie.

Sure enough, this second line of action I took, after my original, anxiety-producing failure, resulted in considerable profits for me. And the knowledge and experience I've built up in the oil and gas field have been the source of much of my present fortune. The lesson I learned by moving ahead and putting my worry to work for me is simple: It's alway better to have a small piece of something good than complete or substantial ownership of something bad. But I doubt that I would ever have made this lesson a part of my life if I hadn't decided to use my anxiety as a spur for action, rather than as an excuse for giving up.

2. COMMUNICATING YOUR CONCERN TO SUBORDINATES WILL MAKE YOU A BETTER MANAGER. Another early business venture I got into involved the purchase of an apartment house in San Francisco. I had made a little money, over and above our daily budgeting requirements, from a radio show I had, and I was approached by a real estate man who said he had been impressed by a talk I gave to a local businessmen's club. He suggested that I could make some money by investing in an apartment building, but I said, "I don't know anything about business."

"I'll shepherd it through for you," he replied, quite generously I thought. "I'll not only see you get a good buy, but I'll handle the books so you won't have to worry about rent collections, tenant problems, and such things. Every six months or so, I'll give you a report."

It sounded great, so I invested as much as I could scrape together and bought two small apartment houses. But I never seemed to make any money. The records he sent to me always showed an alarming number of vacancies, and the best I could do in any accounting period was to lose money.

"You know, this doesn't seem like such a good investment," I told him one day.

But he replied: "It's just the times, just a downswing in the economy. Things will pick up before long."

"Okay," I said. "You're the boss. You know what you're doing."

But one day my wife, Lois, and I were driving around the city, and we realized we had never even visited the apartments that we owned, so we went over, browsed around, and talked to some tenants. To our surprise, we learned that all the apartments were occupied and apparently had been for months. Yet once again, when we received the next report from our real estate expert, there were many vacancies indicated on the sheet.

So I called him on the phone and said, "Hey, we drove over to that building and the place was full!"

He seemed confused and tried to make some excuse about giving the units to some people for nothing so that the apartment as a whole would look attractive and in demand. But on further questioning, it was clear this explanation wouldn't stand up. Finally, he broke down and admitted he had been cheating me. He actually cried and asked for my forgiveness, and strangely enough, I didn't feel vengeful. I was just shocked. It was a tremendous blow to discover that an apparently honest upright businessman would do something like that to me.

It took me a while to recover from this experience, but when I finally could objectively evaluate what had happened, I didn't decide to distrust everyone and anyone. I knew I could never find success in business dealings if

I took that approach. Instead, I realized that you should no more encourage people to take advantage of you in the marketplace than you should entice someone to steal your car by leaving your key in the ignition. With my hands-off attitude in that real estate venture, I was partly to blame for what had happened. In a way, I had invited the theft by not expressing my concern about my investment and maintaining a presence around the person who was managing my affairs.

I have never since put my total trust in anyone without letting him know I was around—not in a suspicious or distrustful way, but just as a very interested onlooker. Or, as the British used to say, "We show the flag in any enterprise."

For example, I own several ranches in Australia, and I've hired several top, reliable people to run them for me. One man who oversees the property has been with me for nineteen years, and I have an excellent accountant in a nearby city who checks all the books and tax returns. I have every reason to think everything is being done to guard my interest in those ranches, but I still make at least one long and arduous trip to the Outback every year. Because that property is such an important part of my whole estate, I want my employees to know I'm vitally interested in what they're doing. I break my neck to get down there, and I also keep in touch by letter and phone. There's never any overwhelming crisis that requires my presence, but I learned from those apartment buildings in San Francisco that it's important for me to make the 17,000-mile trip so that I can sit down with my ranch manager and let him know I care.

3. A LITTLE TENSION CAN MEAN A LARGE SUCCESS. If you've got an important speech or presentation or other

project on the horizon, it's important to feel a certain amount of tension and anxiety. If I don't feel a little nervous before I stand up to speak to an audience, I know I'm likely to be missing some of the sharpness and edge I like to have before a group. Worry is the little threat or whip that makes you perform better, like the race horse that prances and sweats before the starter's gun goes off. If you saw some old milk-wagon nag standing calmly next to the skittish thoroughbred, you certainly wouldn't place your bet on the animal that showed the least anxiety.

George Jessel used to have these words for the director who got upset about the tantrums of a temperamental actress: "Look, if you want somebody for your picture who won't blow up, I have an Aunt Minnie who lives in Minneapolis and she'll come right out here and I guarantee she'll never be temperamental. . . ."

Most of us come up to an important event with a heightened sense of anticipation, and this means our nerves are on edge. But this can help you as long as your worry doesn't get out of hand. Someone once told me: "It's not important that you have butterflies in your stomach. What is important is that you teach them to fly in formation."

I've only known a couple of people in show business who never seemed to have a moment of concern in their professional lives. One is Perry Como and the other is Ethel Merman. As one story goes, Ethel was standing in the wings just before one of her Broadway openings, that most critical moment in the life of a stage performer. Someone said, "You don't seem at all nervous." And she replied, "Why should I? I know my lines!"

Perry's and Ethel's coolness under pressure is unusual,

though. Most people experience that uncertain stomach, that sense of inadequacy and fear. But look forward to it, because the right amount of tension is often a prerequisite for a big success.

4. YOUR GREATEST WORRY CAN SPUR YOU ON TO YOUR GREATEST ACHIEVEMENT. I've faced a number of major disasters or tragedies, any of which might qualify as my greatest worry. But the one that was perhaps most decisive for my career was the time I got fired and was forced to make my own way as a freelancer.

When I was in my mid-twenties and had managed to accumulate considerable experience as a radio announcer at two world's fairs, I was offered the job of radio director of the Golden Gate International Exposition in San Francisco. Because of my youth, there was some resentment of the job I'd been given, and much of the criticism I received came from the fair's general manager, Harris De Haven Connick.

In Connick's eyes, I could do nothing right. He called me into his office one day and gave me an up-to-date evaluation of my performance: "Mr. Linkletter, I regret to say that in my opinion your work has been dull, without imagination, and more or less useless. Now let's get on the ball for our big opening show!"

I knew I had a ways to go before I measured up in Connick's eyes, so I focused all my energies on coming up with a surefire opening day promotional gimmick. With a longstanding colleague, Clyde Vandeburg, I arranged for Richard Halliburton, the famous author, to go to China, purchase a large junk, and then sail back and arrive at the Golden Gate as a principal feature of the opening day's ceremonies.

When Connick heard about the idea, he called me into

his office and as I stood in front of him (he never invited me to take a seat when I was in his presence), he told me he thought the whole idea was silly. I could feel my temper rising, but I managed to limit my reply, "What do *you* have in mind for opening day, Mr. Connick?"

"Something with a little *real* imagination," he said patronizingly and waved his hand toward a window overlooking the Golden Gate Bridge. "See those suspension cables holding up the world's longest bridge?"

"Yes."

"Ever *hear* those cables when the wind from Hawaii blows through them?"

"I guess I have," I replied. "But what has that to do with opening a world's fair?"

"That is music you hear, Mr. Linkletter," Connick said, smiling condescendingly. "Each cable has a different tension that produces its own note. All you have to do is pick out the eight notes on the scale, if you know them, and put a microphone on each one of the cables wherever it occurs across that bridge."

"And then?" I asked numbly.

"You run wires from the microphones to a keyboard console, and on opening day, you get someone like Artur Rubinstein to sit down and play 'California Here I Come!' on the world's largest Aeolian harp!" He beamed, apparently picturing the scene in living color in his imagination. "What do you think of *that*?" he demanded.

"Mr. Connick," I said, almost automatically. "I think you're nuts."

The smile disappeared. "And I *know*, Mr. Linkletter," he said, "that you're fired."

I spent most of my ride home trying to recover my self-esteem. It's a terrible thing, to get fired. At first, you can't believe it's happened. Then, a wave of embarrassment sets in. All sorts of hostile thoughts went through my mind about Connick, and then I started in on myself. I had handled the whole thing badly, I thought. I should have avoided that confrontation. Then I tried to gather my inner forces before I saw Lois. How would I tell her about my failure?

As it happened, she was too quick for me to worry about how I'd bring the subject up. She looked up in surprise as I walked in the door and said, "You're early."

"I've got great news," I said bravely. I wanted to bolster my own self-confidence as much as I wanted to ease into the bad news with her.

"What is it?" she asked.

"I've decided the time has come to make it big," I announced grandly.

"What do you mean?"

"I'm going to freelance."

"What about your job?" That was just like Lois, to get right to the point. We had only been married about two years, but she could read me like a book even then. Our first child, Jack, had just been born, and she was concerned, of course, about the source of the next paycheck.

"My imagination has been stifled long enough," I replied euphemistically.

"You got fired."

"Just before I was going to resign," I responded defensively.

Actually, there was some truth to my statement because I had been getting restless. But the abrupt loss of my job, the involuntary severance of the old umbilical cord of a regular salary, pushed me with a vengeance out into the tough, competitive world of the promotional freelancer. Otherwise, I'm not sure I would have made the leap. Worry about a lack of money and about occupational failure spurred me to the extent that within four weeks of the loss of my job, I was making more money than the fair's president. I became a "packager" who put all the talent and support people together and sold it to sponsors of the fair as a complete show. As I got the accounts of more private exhibitors, my earnings jumped from $500 to $2000 a month—a respectable sum in 1939 and twice as much as that ultimate goal I had set for myself a few years back as a radio announcer.

One of my freelance jobs was my first network radio account, the "World's Fair Party" sponsored by the Roma Wine Company. This was a live audience participation and interview show from the fair's Food and Beverage Building and was the forerunner of my "People Are Funny" and "House Party" programs, which later brought me so much success on radio and television.

So the worries and insecurities that hit me after getting fired actually spurred me to accomplishments I'd only vaguely dreamed about before I was so roughly thrust out on my own. The same might be true for you, but the first step is always to resolve to make that big worry go to work for you. When you decide to transform your negative experience into a positive one, the sky is the limit for what you can achieve.

5. THE SECRET OF RESILIENCE IS "FACING THE PIT" OF TOTAL FAILURE. If you've lost your job, that may depress you for a few days or even weeks, but most people can eventually gather their inner resources and make some sort of comeback. But sometimes a total career disaster

strikes that threatens to ruin you completely, for all time. If you can rebound from an experience like that, you'll have a rock-bottom reference point for resiliency in the less serious challenges you'll face in the future.

I faced the pit of total career annihilation in 1942, after I had become a well-known radio personality in the San Francisco area. Everything seemed to be going well for me, until I passed a sidewalk newsstand and did what must have been the most dramatic double take in history. The newspaper headlines that caught my eye and riveted me to the spot screamed in large, bold-faced type, ART LINKLETTER INDICTED.

I couldn't believe it. I thought a rival station must have set up some sort of gag to break through my on-the-air display of unflappability. But I grabbed a paper and ducked into the nearest office building lobby to read the story, and sure enough, it was all true. I had been indicted by a federal grand jury for lying about my birthplace, falsely claiming to be an American citizen, illegally voting in an election, and stating that I had never been out of the United States. I could be sentenced to five years in prison and fined $5000.

All the charges were true, and my heart sank so low I wanted to climb into the nearest sewer and never come out again. I had made the very human mistake of wishing something—my American citizenship—were true and then convincing myself of its truth. I had actually been born in Moose Jaw in Canada's Saskatchewan province and was adopted as a very young baby by John and Mary Linkletter. (My real name was Arthur Gordon Kelly.) They got me from my mother, an unmarried young woman named Effie Brown who had been unable to care properly for me.

Because I had lived in the United States since I was a year old, I felt like an American and even convinced myself that I was an American, but of course, it wasn't so. Still, my own self-deception had made me careless. I had given my birthplace as Lowell, Massachusetts, on my security clearance application for my shortwave work. I had voted in a United States election. To top it all off, I had let my conscience get the best of me at one point, faced the fact that I had no proof of citizenship, and applied to the bureau of United States Immigration Service for American citizenship. On the application I stated I'd never been out of the country but had genuinely forgotten I'd taken a short trip to South America as a teenager, working as a cadet on a passenger liner out of New York.

My world came crashing down around me. My career had been ascending, and the heights of fame and achievement were now in sight. But it seemed that all might be over. There was the shame of a federal conviction and possible jail sentence. How could I possibly come back after such a disaster?

I'm not a worrywart, but you can bet I was as anxious as I'll ever be as I was ushered into the federal marshal's office, booked, fingerprinted, and photographed. We posted bail and a court appearance was set before Federal Judge Michael J. Roche.

At the hearing, my lawyer, Bill O'Brien, asked for probation, and then the judge addressed me directly. "Perhaps your success has made you feel that it is not necessary to obey the law."

"I never had any such thought, your honor," I replied.

"If I were to excuse you, it would set a precedent."

It seemed the worst was about to happen. I stood

numbly as he continued. "This is not a case for probation. Probation denied." No ad lib or fast reply could turn the situation to my advantage now. I was facing the pit, the end of my life as I'd known it. Already, I was wondering what it would be like when I got out of jail, an ex-convict looking for a job.

"I fine you $500 or six months in jail," the judge said. I could hardly believe my ears. But then he continued, "I am, with this sentence, extending to you the charity of this country."

Teetering on the edge of destruction, something or Someone had pulled me back at the last moment. All of a sudden the judge seemed kind and compassionate. He was explaining that he knew my motives were sound, and he felt I'd make a good citizen. He had denied me probation because a probationary period would have delayed my citizenship.

I don't know when I've ever been happier or more relieved, and I learned quite a few lessons that morning that I've carried with me throughout my life. For one thing, I've never taken my citizenship for granted since then, because I'd almost been denied it. I also never make any unwarranted assumptions about important things in my life. In fact, I'm now conscientious to the point of being tiresome, sometimes, about checking things out before I act.

But most important of all, I'm more resilient when I face lesser problems and setbacks than the complete loss of a thriving career. I certainly wouldn't encourage others to precipitate such a total disaster to learn this lesson. But should you face the pit of complete failure, the inevitable anxiety that grips you will stand you in good stead later. The combat veteran who has once demonstrated heroism under fire can be counted on to keep a cool head when the guns begin to roar a second time.

6. BEWARE THE WORRY THAT LEADS YOU TO WALLOW IN GUILT. So far, I've concentrated on how you can use worry to your advantage, but there are limits to healthy anxiety. Sometimes, an especially devastating personal tragedy may hit you, and worry may linger in the form of guilt. I confronted just that problem when my daughter, Diane, died back in 1969 at the age of twenty. Diane had everything going for her: looks, a bright future as a performer, a warm personality. And besides all that, she was my baby, the youngest child of five, and my dearest joy in life.

I was waiting to address the Air Force Academy's graduating class at Colorado Springs, when my lawyer, Will Layman, called me from California to tell me that Diane was dead. She had been killed as the result of a fall or jump from the sixth-floor balcony of her Hollywood apartment above Sunset Strip. There was no measurable amount of any drug found in her body after her death. But I can only speculate from information I got later from her friends that she had experimented with LSD in the past and may have experienced a flashback from a previous mind-blowing acid trip.

A young man had been with Diane the evening she died. He told the police and my private investigators that she had begun to feel something was wrong while she was cooking dinner. She telephoned her brother, Robert, and expressed fear that she was starting a recurring bad trip. But her companion got on the phone and told my son not to worry, that he had Diane in sight all the time and would make certain that she didn't hurt herself.

Robert and Diane, my two youngest, had always been

close, and Robert hung up the phone in an unsettled frame of mind. He knew that Diane had gone through one other LSD recurrence, and even though he trusted the young man who was with her, he decided to go to her apartment, just to be safe. In the meantime, Diane left her friend in the living room to go into the kitchen and check the oven. No one saw her alive after that. Whatever it was must have hit her as she crossed the kitchen. She detoured to a sliding-glass door onto the balcony, and within seconds she had plunged to her death. The chocolate cookies she was making lay unbaked beside the oven.

My world fell to pieces around me. The agony of the loss is indescribable. But after the initial shock wore off, my overriding emotion was anger. I was angry at drug pushers, angry at the climate in this country that allowed them to flourish. Speeches I made and statements I gave to the press reflected this anger. "It was murder," I told the Los Angeles Times. "She was murdered by the people who manufacture and sell LSD."

My anger and bitterness was so apparent that a prominent motion picture and television star (and a good personal friend) approached me with a bizarre proposal, to say the least. "Do these pushers, this filth, get justice even if they're caught?" he asked me. "No, they have money to pay fines. They get off with a light sentence or probation, and hours later they're back down near the school or over in the park selling to our kids. Art, let's five or six of us put in $10,000 each, set up a bank account, and hire some top private investigators to identify the key pushers, the ones who are essential to all the smaller operators. We'll only go for the big shots without whom a lot of the street business would fold."

"And then what?" I asked. "Turn them over to the police or the D.A. for prosecution?"

"No," he said, his voice dropping almost to a whisper. "We go out and kill them ourselves."

I stared at him in shocked silence. This gentle, warm-hearted man, who would never permit such words and ideas to be put into one of his scripts, was completely serious. "We . . . we couldn't do anything like that," I replied, aghast at the bizarre idea.

"Why not? We're all so well known that we'd be above suspicion. The very idea that we would do anything like that would be considered so absurd that no one would even dream of investigating us. And the good we would do; others would be afraid to take their places because they'd think there was some kind of mob war going on. We'd save not only our kids, Art, but thousands of other youngsters throughout this whole area."

My anger ran deep, but not that deep. It wasn't that I felt a deep sense of Christian charity for those who had given Diane LSD, but the issues that were facing me came into clearer focus after this conversation. I knew, for one thing, I had to draw the line at violent revenge. And I could see my excessive anger wasn't getting me anywhere either. Underlying all my feelings during this difficult period was a sense of guilt—a tendency to blame myself and ask where, as a parent, I had gone wrong.

I played over and over in my mind conversations I'd had with Diane and her friends before her death. One jilted boyfriend had warned me about Diane's drug use and the fast crowd she was running with, but I chalked that up to this boy's distorted, jealous ravings. Why hadn't I listened? Shouldn't I have seen what was going on? But I had confronted her about drugs, and she had denied any experimentation. She had even told her mother that there were some parties she was afraid to attend because of heavy drug use. So what could I do, when my daughter stood there and told me she wasn't doing anything wrong?

It was during this state of frustration that I received a letter from Dr. Norman Vincent Peale. He urged me to think hard about the real meaning of my daughter's death. Diane's death was not without God's purpose, he wrote. My loss, far from being an event that ruined my effectiveness, should drive me to become even more effective in helping others. I would be motivated as no other crusader in this cause. He, in effect, suggested that I launch a compassionate program to help others with the same problems.

That was the main thing I needed to fight free of the quagmire of anger and guilt that was immobilizing me. I hit the lecture circuit to speak against drug use, and in counseling sessions and by supporting anti-drug movements, I became a leader in the war against drug abuse. There were times, especially at the beginning, when I had to fight back the tears as I discussed Diane's experience on lecture platforms. But I had learned from Dr. Peale and from later conversations with Billy Graham that when worry and anxiety threaten to turn you into a perpetually angry, guilt-ridden person, it's time to take action to change the destructive course your life is taking.

To push these debilitating anxieties and emotions behind you, there are two essential steps. First of all, you have to decide you're not going to be consumed by guilt and worry. It's a simple act of will. And secondly, you have to immerse yourself immediately in some other rewarding, meaningful pursuit.

I often tell families I'm counseling, "After you've lost a child, you are consumed by guilt. You search for any reason that confirms your suspicion that the tragedy was your fault. You aren't objective, and your consuming desire is to punish yourself. The tendency is to exaggerate small disagreements and failures with the child so that you can prove to yourself that you're the one who's in the wrong."

In one family I know quite well, the son wanted to join the Marine Corps, and his father thought that was a marvelous thing. But the boy was lost and killed in a routine landing maneuver as a pilot stationed in Hawaii. The mother, who had disapproved of the military thing from the beginning, never forgave the father for his part in encouraging their son. She aggravated his own sense of guilt time and time again. She almost ruined their marriage by dredging up her grudge when routine arguments about money or anything else would pop up. "That's what I'd expect from you—you, who would kill our own son!" she'd say.

Another young man I knew was killed flying his own plane, and the mother blamed the father for even driving the son to the airfield where he was to take off. There seems to be an almost diabolical streak that lies in each of us, to keep playing over and over the tragedies we experience, in an effort to understand them and perhaps come to some peace within ourselves. But instead of resolving anything, we just keep reopening old wounds, accusing ourselves or our loved ones of being too strict or not strict enough, too distant in the relationship or not distant enough.

Because many people are aware of Diane's story, I often become a lightning rod for those with similar problems. And I tell them the two-step process I've found to work: Decide to push worry and guilt away. Get involved in helping others. And as people come to me and ask my advice, they serve as a constant sorrowful reminder to me of my own continuing fight against self-recrimination. I suppose that's part of the price I pay for following my own and Dr. Peale's advice not to wallow in anger and guilt, but to move ahead and leave those destructive emotions where they belong—in the past.

PART THREE

How to Influence Other People

CHAPTER 6

Build an Old Boy/Old Girl Network

When we embark on the road to success, we often stress developing a high degree of skill in some field and getting organized, almost like a machine, so that our expertise can be used to the best advantage. Ideas and methods dominate our lives. Ironically, the most important factor in success—good relationships with other people—often gets ignored.

I would go so far as to say the single most important factor in success is your contacts with key people. They refer business to other individuals whom they know and like. The better someone knows you, the more likely it is that he'll remember you and recommend you for a job opening he hears about. This is what used to be known as the "old boy network"—a name that must be changed, in light of the recent influx of women into the job market, to the "old boy/old girl network."

One of the most dramatic recent examples of the importance of contacts in business involves my son, Jack. He has been the national president of the Young Presidents Organization, to which thousands of young presidents from all over the country belong. As a result of Jack's contacts, at Linkletter Enterprises we have found that whatever business problem we face, we can always find someone in the YPO who can help us find an answer. If we're wrestling with a particularly tough, unusual problem with some financial arrangement, Jack or I can call Joe Smith who runs a business in Atlanta and who has faced a similar difficulty. He'll either tell us how to solve the problem on the phone or may actually send a man out for a couple of days to spend some time with us.

Another man who impressed me with the way he built up personal contacts was the late Robert Kriendler, the president of the 21 Club in New York City. He and his wife Florence went to Greece on vacation with Lois and me one year. But while Lois and I were off seeing some ancient ruins near Athens, Bob and Florence, who had perhaps the most successful restaurant in the world, sat in their hotel room and churned out about 350 "wish you were here" postcards to important customers around the world. They recognized that the key to success is people, and no matter how smart you are or how businesslike in handling money, you're asking for trouble unless you cultivate friendships and personal contacts.

I'm not suggesting, however, that these relationships be manipulative or that you merely use people for what they can do for you. The only meaningful contact is one that involves a genuine, giving personal interaction. You may want another person to help you in business, but you must also be willing to help him and to spend time getting to know his interests and needs. You can't fake that kind of a concerned attitude for any period of time. It has to be real and heartfelt, or it's best not to try to establish the relationship at all.

Spend a few moments now thinking about your own network of friends and acquaintances. Just to see what kind of friend you are, jot down the names of those you would consider close friends, and then people who are casual friends in the sense that you may not see them regularly, but you feel you can rely on them for help in a crisis or for a favorable business recommendation or reference.

Beside each name, indicate how often you get in touch with this person. You'll probably be shocked at how you've neglected some people whom you actually consider close to you. When I do this exercise, I sometimes find I've let several months slip by without dropping a card or making a phone call to some of my dearest acqaintances. It may be the fact that I live far away from some of these individuals or that I get too heavily involved in my own work. Whatever the reason, I know there's no excuse, and I'll frequently pick the phone right up and spend a few minutes in conversation with this person I've neglected. Or, more often, I'll write a note on my old typewriter out in the backyard, while I'm getting some sun next to the pool. I also rely on postcards, like Bob Kriendler did. "Postcard power" is something I'd encourage you to cultivate because it is convenient, inexpensive, and you can put down a quick thought or two and drop it in the mail in just a minute or so. Carry a few with you on trips, as I do, and use "dead time" as you're waiting for an airplane or train to keep in touch with those people who are so important to you.

Another painless way to keep in touch is through business lunches. I almost always schedule the noontime meal with someone who has something to discuss about one of my businesses or, more often, just with people whom I like and who interest me for one reason or another. I've had some of the most stimulating discussions of my life with authors, educators, scientists, architects, politicians, and sports figures at some of these lunches. And the ideas that are generated in these conversations have been invaluable to me in both business and personal projects in recent years.

I believe you're wasting your time if you eat alone, even if you're reading a book over your meal. It's not necessary to have an expense account to arrange a lunch with a friend you haven't seen in a while or to get to know someone you've been wanting to talk to. There are also plenty of professional lunches with interesting speakers in most cities. Find out where they are held and broaden your horizons once in a while!

Just bemoaning the fact that you haven't been keeping up with friends isn't enough. Most people are quite adept at beating their breasts for a few minutes and then reverting back to their old habit of giving their personal contacts a low priority. To get out of your rut, you have to take action right now. Pick up the phone and call a friend for a lunch date or for some evening event at which you and your spouses can get together for a chat. As far as letter-writing goes, set aside a half hour at a convenient time—perhaps just before you go to bed at night, or maybe as you're watching some television program that doesn't require all your attention. Write a couple of postcards or a short letter, and don't set your sights too high. You'll never get to first base if you think you have to write a ten-page tome to make up for the months you haven't written.

While it's important to revive old friendships, it's also essential for you to broaden your personal contacts. The more people you know, the more possibilities you have to get involved in interesting and successful projects. The next step to consider is how you can make successful initial contacts with people and improve your chances for establishing firm friendships, which are the foundation for most success.

CHAPTER 7

From Shyness to Self-Promotion

I'm constantly amazed at the number of people who, when you get them into a frank, personal conversation, will admit they're basically shy. One of the friends I had always thought to be a swinging extrovert confessed to me in a reflective mood: "You know, Art, I really get cold feet every time I have to meet someone new. I can tell jokes and horse around like mad with a crowd of people I know, but I'd rather stay at home with a book than try to make conversation at a dinner party with a stranger."

This person is really saying, "I don't want to meet new people because I'm afraid they won't accept me." Unless you're a misanthrope who can't stand people in the first place, your shyness reflects nothing more than your lack of confidence in yourself. You should be well on your way to overcoming this lack of self-confidence after thinking through your strengths and weaknesses and doing the exercises outlined in the first two chapters. But keep in mind a few principles for overcoming shyness that can help you feel more natural in reaching out to strangers and prompting yourself in unusual situations.

1. PUT THE OTHER PERSON ON STAGE AND CONCENTRATE

ON HIS NEEDS. I know a young man whose voice always quavered when he started to speak, even before a very small group. The usual butterflies that most people have would practically strangle him, and his breath would grow so short that sometimes he couldn't choke out more than a couple of words in a row. After he had spoken for a minute or two and warmed up to his audience, he found that he could communicate more freely. It was that excruciating first minute or two that he was determined to master so that he could improve his poise in getting his ideas across to others.

In analyzing his difficulty, he finally realized that he was most nervous when he was concentrating on himself and his own image. In a way, he actually became a member of his audience during that first minute or so as he stood aside and watched his own performance very critically. But then he found that he relaxed more when he switched his focus and began to put the needs and interests of his listeners on stage instead of himself. *Their* reactions became his *primary* target.

Concentrating on the other fellow's problems is also one of the primary keys to successful salesmanship. In my book *How to Be a Supersalesman*, I mentioned an incident involving my good friend Charles Luckman, former president of Lever Brothers. When he was first starting out, Chuck got a job with Colgate-Palmolive-Peet as a draftsman at $125 a month, and one of his first jobs was to design a brochure for soap displays at stores. His boss said the layout was lousy, but Chuck insisted it would work and asked permission to try it out at one of the local grocers'. Naturally, the boss sent him to one of the toughest, meanest sections of town, and everyone sat back to watch him fall on his face. If he had been worrying about his own image and had allowed himself to become timid, he probably would have failed.

But instead of focusing on how hard and impossible his own job was, he zeroed in on the needs of the storeowner. The man was negative at first because he had never been successful in selling soap in his shop. But Chuck rolled up his sleeves and for the next hour helped him to rearrange his displays so that the cigarettes and other fast-moving items were away from the front counter, and some sweet-smelling but slow-selling soap was closer to the front (with an attractive brochure designed by Luckman). The shopkeeper was astounded to find a company representative who thought of *his* needs and became a good customer.

Such experiences have convinced me that anyone who develops excessive nervousness or mild panic at the thought of encountering new people should go through a little personal ritual before the talk or meeting. First, give careful thought to the interests and needs of those you'll be dealing with. Decide how you can help or encourage them. You have experience and knowledge that no one else possesses, so sort out what will be most relevant to the group or individual you'll be talking to, and focus on that particular point as you're speaking. Finally, whenever you feel yourself slipping back, in the sense that you're watching your own performance rather than putting the spotlight on others, make a conscious effort to get back into the position of the attentive, supportive onlooker. Most of you who follow this approach will find that you have changed from a shrinking violet to an exciting personality whose confidence blooms every time you're asked to express your opinion on a subject.

2. THE WINDS OF HUMOR CAN BLOW AWAY THE CLOUDS

OF SELF-CONSCIOUSNESS. When you're scheduled to meet someone who seems particularly formidable, such as a person who is interviewing you for a job, try imagining that person in a ridiculous outfit. My old basketball coach would always tell the team just before an important game, "Just remember, those guys on the other team pull their pants on the same way you do!" Carrying this image one step further, you might imagine the impressive person you're meeting wearing an Easter bunny suit or as a small child. Or as he begins to speak to you, try to pair him with some animal caricature, such as a braying mule or a squawking chicken. Look out at an audience and visualize them all sitting there in their underwear! Far from being immobilized by your own timidity, you'll probably find you have to fight to control your laughter.

3. RELIEVE THE PRESSURE ON ANY MEETING BY REMEMBERING THERE WILL ALWAYS BE ANOTHER DAY. Placing too much importance on a specific meeting with an individual or a group causes tension. Some personal encounters may change your life for the better, but I'm convinced that they *never* irreparably change it for the worse. What it all boils down to is this: If you fail to impress somebody, so what? In the long run, what difference does it make? If you've just had one chance to influence an important person or cement an important liaison or friendship and things don't work out, there's still every reason to believe that you'll get another chance with someone else at some future point. And undoubtedly your failure in this instance will teach you something and prepare you to handle your next opportunity more adeptly.

People who fail in life are those who allow one important setback or unpleasant conversation to undercut their self-confidence and force them into a shell of shyness.

Instead of saying, "I'm going to do better next time because I've learned this and this," they refuse to risk exposing themselves to the possibility of rejection a second time. You've got very little to lose and a great deal to gain from any new acquaintances you make, so plunge into your interviews, new client calls, and social events with boldness. Make your life as exciting as any high-seas adventure. You can do it if you just make up your mind to it!

4. TURN EVERY NEW ACQUAINTANCESHIP INTO A GAME, THE OBJECT OF WHICH IS TO GET THE OTHER PERSON INTERESTED IN YOU. The first step in any effective conversation is to listen to the other person and show a genuine interest in him. But after you've listened, feel free to start talking about yourself a little bit. Mention things you've read recently in the newspapers that have influenced your opinion one way or another. Then, get more personal. Lace the points you're making with stories and anecdotes from your own personal experience. The secret of good public speaking is putting across illustrative stories to make your points. And in a one-on-one personal discussion, you can make your points not only more effectively with anecdotes from your own experience, but you can also inform the other person who you are and what you've done in the most palatable way possible. Your companion should go home knowing enough about you to remember you when you get in touch in the future. And if he believes you're interested in his activities as well, he'll look forward to that future meeting as much as you will.

If you regard a meeting with a stranger as a challenge or a game, the object of which is to get him interested in you as a person, you'll be less inclined to worry about the image you're projecting. Instead of focusing on your deficiencies—that attitude is at the root of most shyness —you'll be devoting all your energies to influencing that other person to like and respond to you. You'll be selling yourself in the most attractive manner possible, and that kind of self-promotion is the perfect antidote to any sort of shyness.

CHAPTER 8

The Close-Aide Principle

One of the biggest mistakes junior executives-on-the-make commit is to shower all their attention and energies on the top person in an organization, and to forget to build relationships with secretaries and close aides. I found, for example, in my early working experience when I had to sell myself to a prospective employer, that it was essential to make friends with the private secretary of the guy. If I was sitting in the outer office, waiting to see her boss, I'd make it a point to be pleasant and friendly to her and sell myself to her in much the same way I'd try to sell myself to the boss.

As a result, when I would call up in an emergency and tell her I needed to get through immediately to her employer, I could count on her being helpful. Instead of harboring some negative feelings toward me, she would think, There's that nice Mr. Linkletter on the phone, and I'm going to do everything I can to get him through to Mr. so-and-so.

In addition to facilitating communications with their superiors, close aides can also reinforce the idea that you're a good guy if your name ever comes up in conversation. Major business decisions are rarely made in a vacuum these days, and people with titles like "assistant to," "deputy chief," and "executive secretary" wield more power than ever before. It's essential, therefore, as you plot your blueprint for success in life, that you take into account not only the chief executive or branch head, but also the support troops that have input into that person's decisions.

I recently had lunch with a lobbyist who represents a major group of businesses in Washington. This man, though, rarely sees members of the House or Senate. Instead, he spends all his time with their legislative aides and administrative assistants. He takes them out to lunch, educates them in economic matters they might be wrestling with, and generally helps them understand the business community from his clients' point of view. As a result, he knows he'll get their employers, the various congressmen and senators, to vote in his favor 75 percent of the time even though he never communicates with them directly.

Because these ideas may not seem immediately applicable to you unless you spend some time thinking about your own business contacts, take a few moments right now to consider your own situation. If you're employed by a large corporation, list those superiors who have the most influence over your future. Beside their names write down the people who have the most say when these executives make decisions that affect you. If you're self-employed or spend most of your time working with clients, jot down those contacts who account for most of your business and include their subordinates too.

As you wrote down these names, you probably realized that many people you deal with on a regular—even daily —basis get very little personal attention from you. You may recall times when you were obnoxious, too demand-ing, or even condescending. The surest way to alienate an executive secretary is to treat her like a menial. And if you alienate her, chances are that your messages to her boss will get delayed or perhaps even lost.

In recommending that you spend time cultivating people in subordinate roles, I'm not suggesting that you just try to manipulate or use them. Motives are always mixed, and I wouldn't be truthful if I suggested that you should completely ignore your own interests in getting on the good side of secretaries and assistants-to. On the other hand, if the only thing you're interested in is fur-thering your own ends, these subordinates will quickly see through to your basic selfishness, and you'll likely be in a worse position with them than if you had just ignored them completely.

To influence an aide, it's necessary to demonstrate a genuine concern for him or her personally, just as you would behave toward a person in a nonbusiness environ-ment with whom you want to establish a friendship. The impression you make on top-level executives, whether in business or government, is likely to be a group impression of yourself. Each person you meet in an office sees a slightly different side of your personality, and there's much more communication than you may realize in put-ting together those piecemeal impressions to get an idea of what you're like as a whole person. In this regard, I'm reminded of the book *Rector of Justin* by Louis Auchin-closs, about how a number of different people viewed the personality of a certain educator. From one person's point of view, he was a genial Mr. Chips, but from another viewpoint, he more closely resembled an aca-demic Captain Bligh. It almost seemed as though the

author were writing about several entirely different people, until at the end of the book you realized that all these
impressions were different facets of the same personality.

You face the same kind of multiple personality analysis
every time you walk into an office, so be sure that you
remain aware of the whole impression you're creating,
and not just the image that is perceived by one or two
individuals.

CHAPTER 9

Listeners Rule
the World of Conversation

Being a good listener is the most essential part of being a good conversationalist. And being a good conversationalist is necessary for anyone who wants to enhance his or her chances of success in life.

I was particularly struck by how important listening is during a recent encounter I had with California's Governor Jerry Brown. I've been active in the Republican Party for a number of years, and my attitude toward Democratic Governor Brown naturally had been colored by critical disagreement with some of his policies. He and I were picked as the two principal speakers at a large dinner party for narcotics officers, and I must admit I didn't quite know what to expect of him. We had never met, and I had an idea we wouldn't get to know each other much better at this event.

But I was in for a surprise. Brown stopped by to say hello to me, and I expected he was just showing me a perfunctory courtesy and would soon move on, but he didn't. He kept standing beside me, asking probing, intelligent questions about my attitude toward drug abuse. For the five minutes that we talked, he gave me his total, undivided attention. He didn't look around but looked directly into my eyes. He acted as though we were completely alone, without another soul anywhere in hearing. A number of people were eavesdropping on our conversation, but the young governor wasn't making any statements for their benefit. I can always tell when a conversation with me is actually directed toward onlookers. There's a certain expansive rhetoric and perhaps a sightly glazed or shifty look in the eyes. But there was none of that with Brown. We might as well have been in a cocoon, all by ourselves, despite the confusion of people milling around, taking their seats for the dinner.

That encounter with Jerry Brown was a dramatic lightning bolt for me. I realized that every principle I'd ever advocated about effective listening in conversation had been present in his approach to me. He really seemed to care about what I had to say, even though we were on opposite sides of the political fence.

Although I had been faintly hostile to him before, I came away from that dinner saying, "Holy smoke, I like him!"

That short talk brought about what is probably the most dramatic change in attitude I've ever experienced toward anyone. Now, even if I am not with him on every political issue, at least I have an admiring, friendly feeling toward him as a person. He had turned me around purely because of his marvelous ability to listen to what I had to say and to make me feel important through his attentiveness.

But even if you spend as much time listening to another person as Jerry Brown did with me, you'll fail to have an impact if you allow your eyes to wander about. So many stimuli make demands on your attention these days that it's often hard to focus on one thing for any period of time, even if that "thing" is another person. You listen for a few seconds to get the drift of the conversation and then start looking around to see what else is going on, or how the room is decorated, or who is saying what to whom. I know one fellow who starts off listening to a companion, and then his eyes get a faraway look as he starts tuning in to bits and pieces of other nearby conversations. Then, if something of particular interest catches his ear, he'll terminate his own discussion as soon as possible so that he can hop into that other conversation for a while.

Another distracting habit is to look at your watch as you're talking to someone. The only messages that you convey in this situation are either that you're bored and want to move on to another topic or partner, or that you've got only a limited amount of time and the person to whom you're talking had better make his comments brief and to the point, or you'll walk away from him. If you are in a hurry, it's best to make that clear at the outset: Look at your watch before you get involved in a discussion and say: "I'm checking my watch because I want to be sure we have a little time together. In a half hour I have to be at such and such a place, and I want to be sure we cover some significant matters before I have to leave." Using this approach, you've been straightforward in telling the other person that you have another commitment and will have to leave shortly. But you've complimented him in stating that the time you're spending with him is valuable to you also.

If you've ever been on the other side of a conversation with someone who suffers from the shifty-eyes or watchwatching malady, you know just how frustrating the experience can be. I remember several discussions with a friend of mine, a wealthy fellow who is probably hyperkinetic in addition to being a business genius. When I'm talking with him, I have the feeling that if I'm not constantly hitting him with amusing quips and entertaining anecdotes, I'm going to lose his attention. Whenever I settle down to a normal pace of conversation, he starts looking around, fiddling with his watch, and giving me other body movement signals that he's losing interest. Then I increase my barrage of jokes and other tidbits, and he focuses on me again. I always feel as though I'm putting on an act for him, using tricks and devices that I'd use to capture the straying attention of an audience of 3000 people; yet there are just the two of us in one corner of a cocktail party.

You've undoubtedly been exposed to all these types of bad listeners, but you may have overlooked some of the same flaws in yourself. The next time you go to a dinner party or some other social function, try observing yourself as you talk with others. Are you listening to everything they say, or do you frequently find you're tuning out, either thinking about something else that's going on around you, or pondering the next thing you plan to say yourself. If you're not paying attention, you're sure to get caught eventually in an embarrassing situation, such as being asked a question about a discussion you weren't even listening to. Even if you think you're covering yourself by listening to just enough of the conversation and monitoring what's going on around you at the same time, your body language—your posture, eyes, and facial movements—will give you away.

I learned early in my career as an interviewer that I could fool adults some of the time, but I could never fool children if I wasn't paying attention to what they were saying. One woman asked me, "How on earth did you get those little kids to talk so openly to you and say all those incredible things they said?"

My response was, "It wasn't the questions I asked—it was the attitude of listening."

I looked right at each child and watched his face and movements closely, no matter how ridiculous his statements might be. I never laughed at him or watched for opportunities to poke fun. Rather, I listened closely and asked sensible questions. As a result, I sometimes got the opportunity to explore a poignant side of the child's personality that might have been lost if I had just settled for the superficial quick laugh.

On one program, I asked a seven-year-old boy what he wanted to be when he grew up, and he said, "I'd like to be an airplane pilot and fly one of those great big jets!"

"Let's pretend you're one of those pilots right now," I said. "You're at the controls of a giant aircraft, flying between Los Angeles and Honolulu at 20,000 feet with a hundred people in the cabin. But then all four engines stop as you're halfway to Honolulu over the ocean. What do you do?"

The little boy looked up at me and asked, "Are you sure that *all* four engines have stopped?"

"Yes," I said, "I'm sorry to tell you that all four engines have stopped."

"Well," he said, "I'd get on the microphone there in the captain's cabin and I'd tell everybody to get into their seatbelts."

"Then what would you do?"

"Oh, I'd put on my parachute and jump out."

The audience howled and stamped their feet at this, but I didn't laugh at all. I looked at him closely, and I could see tears of surprise well up in his eyes. I realized he wasn't making jokes but had something else in mind, so I asked, "Why would you jump out?"

"I'm going for gas—I'm coming back!"

In this situation, you see, I listened closely not only to what the boy said, but I also listened between the lines and examined his body language. His eyes told me something I might have missed entirely if I had been playing to the audience. But because I was focusing on that boy as though no one else were present, I avoided running roughshod over his feelings and also elicited a final comment from him that was better than any joke I might have manufactured. His response provided a touching human quality to our entire discussion.

If you watch and listen with your eyes, your ears, your entire being to every detail of what the other person is saying not only with his voice but with the rest of his body as well, you're going to be the kind of person people love to talk to. Giving someone the compliment of your total attention enhances the quality of your personal relationships and can almost hypnotize the other person so that you can expect the best, most intimate answers and the most interesting conversations that you've ever had in your life. Listening is without a doubt the most important part of informal conversations or selling yourself or some product. If you limit yourself to in-depth, intense talks with one or two people during a social event instead of fragments of a dozen discussions, you'll find your own life becoming richer, and your bonds with other people will become stronger and result in a more satisfying and successful experience for you.

CHAPTER 10

Don't Be Afraid to Be Old-Fashioned

Conformity, deference to authority, and reverence for tradition have now become three of the deadliest sins a free, self-determined, contemporary man or woman can commit. Yet paradoxically, these sins are often an essential part of the formula for success that can lead to the freedom and self-determination most people want so desperately.

Many derisive remarks have been made about the "corporate uniform" of dark suit, conservative tie, and white shirt, for example. But I know from experience—and my personal impressions have been confirmed by books like *Dress for Success* by John T. Molloy—that you'll make the best impression and have the best chance for promotion if you conform to certain standards of appearance. The key thing is to study closely how the top men and women in your company, or the company you're trying to get as an account or client, dress, cut their hair, and otherwise conduct themselves. If you then choose your clothes and hairstyle accordingly, your chances for upward mobility will improve.

Respect for experience and age is another unpopular value these days, but those who act disrespectfully ignore the fact that most top executives who control the movement up the corporate ladder are themselves in their forties and fifties. They've worked hard and fought hard to get where they are, and they expect to be treated with some deference.

Here's an example of what I'm talking about: Henry Kaiser, the great industrialist, was a dear friend of mine whom I got to know when I was hired during World War II to be an executive in charge of building up shipyard morale. At that time, during the early 1940s, he was handling the really big business deals involving American shipping. I was a little wheel and he was a big wheel, but we still became good friends and related to each other on a first-name basis. In later years he began to build an empire in Hawaii.

He would occasionally call me up after midnight to ask me a question about the work and would begin by saying, "This is Henry Kaiser, did I get you up?"

And I'd say, "No, Henry, I had to answer the phone anyway." Then we'd have a laugh and get down to business.

He invited me to spend weekends at his spacious estate at Lake Tahoe, where Howard Hughes, California Governor Goodwin ("Goody") Knight, and other notables sometimes joined us. One time when we were lolling on the shore of the lake, I brought up a subject that had been bothering me.

"Henry, I want to ask you a question," I began. "I've been around your family and closest friends on these weekends here, and it's gradually come to my attention that everybody, including your wife, calls you 'Mr. Kaiser,' and I call you 'Henry.' Now, I'm considerably younger and far less important than you, yet I've presumed to call you by your first name just like you call me 'Art.' I have a first name feeling about you, but I'm wondering what you think?"

"Art," he replied, "here's the way I feel about it: I don't think these other people are calling me 'Mr. Kaiser' in any formal way at all. They're using the word 'mister' like 'colonel' or 'judge' or 'captain.' For them, it's just a little mark of what I've done. But I want you to feel perfectly free to go ahead and call me anything you want."

"I appreciate that very much," I said—and I never called him "Henry" again. I decided that if he thought the word "mister" was a respectful acknowledgment of his accomplishments, the least I could do was to give him the same respect other people did. I knew him well as a friend, but I also regarded him as a great leader. And I had absolutely no feeling that I was retreating from our position of intimacy or deferring completely to his opinions.

Assuming a veneer of refinement and respect is important in any of your business dealings, whether you're working with an equal, a salesman soliciting your account, or one of your employees. Architect Charles Luckman told me about a negotiation he was pursuing with a young vice-president of a major national corporation. Luckman knew the president of the company quite well, but because of protocol considerations, he confined his conversations to the young representative on the West Coast.

The young executive apparently didn't know about Luckman's connections with the top echelons in the company, because he began to give the architect a hard time in their discussions. The younger man was obviously enjoying wielding his power, especially over as prominent a businessman as Chuck. Luckman didn't blow up at this arm-twisting, but instead, on his next trip to New York, he paid a quick visit to his friend, the company president, and described what was happening.

The top executive was aghast and told Luckman, "You'll hear from that fellow shortly."

Sure enough, the West Coast man called within a week and said, in a very friendly way, "Mr. Luckman, I've been waiting to hear from you!"

"You were waiting to hear from me?" Luckman replied.

"Yes, I thought at our last meeting that you were going to decide about the deal and come back to me. I hope there was no misunderstanding."

"Well, I guess I did misunderstand, and I will get back to you," Luckman said. The next day, he went to the young man's office, laid out the deal he wanted, and got just what he asked for. But Luckman didn't gloat or throw his weight around, and he made no mention of the fact that he knew why the atmosphere had changed. He knew he had the power to run over this young guy, demean him, maybe even get him transferred. But he elected, instead, to avoid gloating over his victory and actually thanked the young executive for his help. He knew there was a good chance that he would be working with this man again, in this company or another, and he realized that behaving in a pleasant, businesslike way would be best in the long run, for both of them.

Luckman proved his power to his adversary and thereby won the major battle in these negotiations. But by choosing to back off and open the way to a possible friendship rather than turning the screws on his opponent, he laid the groundwork for further successes with the very man who had originally belittled him.

Luckman's style is one that I'd characterize by the word "grace" or "refinement." Like the medieval knights, he knew certain protocols and niceties must be observed in combat if you hope to maintain a reputation as a fair, high-minded business colleague rather than a dirty, commercial streetfighter. The streetfighter may command fear in his opponents, but they won't choose him when they're looking for long-term career relationships.

Paying attention to proper dress, respectful attitudes toward superiors, and the fair-play traditions of the marketplace may at first blush appear outdated and obsolete, but look again before you cast all these amenities aside. If your goal is success in business and life, it often pays to be old-fashioned.

CHAPTER 11

How to Test Your Talk Power

Communication—especially face-to-face communication with another individual—has been my major occupation in life. As I've tried to hone my own interviewing skills to a fine edge, I've made a number of mistakes, but I've also learned a great deal about influencing other people through the spoken word. To help you benefit from my experiences, I've drawn up the following checklist of conversational ploys and gaffes which I hope will bolster your own "talk power." Some of these lessons came home to me as I stood on a stage or before a radio or television audience, but I've found they apply in private encounters as well. Compare your own approach to communication as you read through this list.

1. BE SENSITIVE TO THE TONE OF YOUR VOICE. You frequently fail to communicate well with others because the tone of your voice or the style with which you put an idea across conveys a different message from that which is in your mind. This problem has bothered me on a number of occasions, and the insidious thing is that usually you're not aware of the difficulty until it's too late.

For example, I've spent thousands of hours in authoritative and dominant positions with audiences as well as in business meetings, and I know that I sometimes come on strong without meaning to be intimidating. As a result, I don't always get the feedback and healthy debate that I need about an idea. I was recently involved in putting together a television show with a young staff, and I scheduled a meeting with the young director-producer to discuss how to reshoot part of the show. Luckily for me, this fellow was completely honest.

"I don't think you're getting the most out of me," he said.

"Why not?" I replied, surprised, because I thought he was doing a fine job.

"You run everything," he said. "You're a strong personality. You speak so decisively and definitely that I sometimes just don't bother to suggest things I think should be done."

"I'm very sorry; I didn't mean to give you that impression at all," I replied. "I want and welcome objections and criticisms and changes, and I value your input. So please tell me anything you disagree with, and I'll listen quite closely. I promise you that because I respect your skills. When we went over that television tape last night, I made a number of suggestions, but I didn't mean for you to take them as ironclad orders. As far as I'm concerned you can do things differently as long as I agree that the final product is all right."

Far from feeling threatened by this man's honesty, I was quite grateful for his comments. He helped me to check my own enthusiasm and tendency to jump in and take charge of the entire project, and he also cleared an obstacle—Art Linkletter—that stood in the way of his own creative energies.

One way to evaluate your tone of voice is to encourage your friends and colleagues to let you know how you're coming across to them. Do you seem unsure of yourself because you overqualify every point you make? Do you appear combative because your voice has a sharp, strident, don't-cross-me edge to it? In becoming more sensitive to your own tone, it's very helpful to listen to yourself periodically on a tape recorder that has been set up at a meeting.

I've often thought I'd love to record some of my friends whom I see socially, such as a man I know who cuts up his wife kiddingly at parties, apparently without even being aware of how it really sounds. I'd like to say, "Martin, I'll bet you've never heard your voice, have you? You know, sometimes you say things you think sound funny, but now listen to them on this tape." If he heard himself with that cutting, strident, almost venomous tone, he would be shocked.

2. ALWAYS DISAGREE AGREEABLY. Look back at that encounter I had with my young producer-director under point number one. Not only did he point out a problem with my tone of voice, but he also did it in the most effective, diplomatic way. Rather than telling me flatly I was wrong, he told me I wasn't getting the most value out of him. He paid me a compliment, in a way, by saying I had a strong personality and then used that opening to get his basic point across.

If you say to anyone, "I've got a better suggestion," or "I think you're wrong," you automatically erect a barrier to further communication. Instead of preventing an open discussion at the outset, try starting off with something like, "I wonder if there's some other way. . . ." Or, "Have we thought of this possibility? . . ." Or perhaps, "Earlier in the discussion someone else said something about such-and-such, and I think we ought to discuss it more. . . ."

Another effective technique in disagreeing agreeably is to restate a point that's just been made by giving the idea your own slant and shading. It's a basic principle in the law that it's better for you to draft your own contract than to allow the other guy to do the original document. It may be more work than just to edit something that's already been written, but you'll be in the stronger position by having set the basic framework for the agreement. The same reasoning applies to business discussions. Redefine or restate the issues as often as possible to direct the discussion toward your viewpoint.

3. MONITOR YOUR BODY LANGUAGE. In that classic western novel, *The Virginian* by Owen Wister, the hero is playing cards in a saloon with his main enemy, Trampas, who gets frustrated and growls, "Your bet, you son-of-a . . ." And the hero responds, "When you call me that, *smile!*"

This confrontation illustrates the importance of body language in any confrontation. You can say almost anything in a conversation, but the real meaning will never get across unless your facial expressions, posture, and gestures are consistent with your words. Few people, for example, like to have a finger shaken at them. Such a gesture, far from merely punctuating a point, conveys hostility, as though a gun were being pointed at you. It's also easy to tell those people who are comfortable and open in their conversations at a party and those who feel ill at ease or threatened. Generally, I've noticed that people who wrap their arms around their waists, turn at an angle away from their companions, and perhaps cross their legs are in effect saying, "I'm worried that you're going to ridicule me, or think I'm stupid, or ask me questions I can't answer." On the other hand, those who face you head-on, incline slightly forward, and open their arms to you are indicating they feel more secure and sure of themselves and are also more interested in you than in their own deficiencies.

Another kind of physical communication, which involves a personal quirk more than any deep-rooted insecurity, is the violation of intimate territory or space. On the beach in Hawaii, I used to have discussions with Louis B. Mayer, the motion picture magnate, and he would invariably move up within four or five inches of my face as he talked. Such crowding was not only intimidating and generated some hostile feelings, but it was also physically unpleasant because he would spray me as he talked. Many people really don't know what they're doing in a case like this, and I think he was one of the oblivious ones. But if you want to infuse your talk with the greatest impact, it's important to watch for and correct such habits or you'll find people are beginning to avoid you.

In a similar vein, I've interviewed people on stage who constantly backed me up so that I finally had to say on the air, "If I have to keep retreating from you, we're going to finish the interview in the alley outside!" Of course, sometimes they were so threatened by the interview that the more I shoved the mike in their faces, the further away they moved. Whatever your personal characteristics, the important thing to remember is this: You have a body language that's every bit as important as your spoken language. So learn to step outside yourself (in a sense) and watch how you perform with people. Check the different parts of your body, one by one—your face, hands, feet, and posture. Then work hard at controlling your body, as much as you control the tone of your voice and the words themselves, so that the message you actually convey will indeed be the message you intend.

4. AVOID CONVERSATIONAL "BUMPERS." The best talkers usually get right to the point, without a long, boring introduction or bumper attached to what they're about to say. It always grates on my sensitivities to turn on the radio and hear an inexperienced interviewer say, "I have a question I'd like to ask you. . . ." or "Now here's a question that comes up from time to time that I think most people would really like to have your answer about. . . ." These preliminaries are either bad habits or just stalling ploys to gain time to think of something really meaningful to say. A good lead in conversation is like a good lead in a newspaper story. Those first words have got to get your listener interested, or he may tune out before you get to the really important things you have to say. Whenever someone says, "I have news for you, Art. . . ." I frequently respond, "Just tell me, and if it's news I'll recognize it."

5. SILENCE STRENGTHENS A POINT, WHILE AUDIBLE PAUSES MANGLE YOUR MESSAGE. I was listening to an interview on a Los Angeles radio station in which the head of a big aerospace company was talking about a new jet that was on the drawing boards. The subject matter was fascinating. The plane could fly at more than 100,000 feet and would get you to Japan in about two hours. But the further the conversation developed, the more annoyed and distracted I became because this man, obviously a top scientist and brilliant executive, kept using the audible pause, "Uh." He would say, "Uh, the plan, uh, is, uh, not, uh, off the drawing boards, but we have,

uh . . ." I found myself counting each uh and ignoring the substance of what he was saying, until finally I switched to another station. He probably thought his speech pattern indicated thoughtful contemplation and careful assessment of each question put to him, but the habit was really destroying the impact of what he had to say.

Another common audible pause that communicates a lack of certainty or even a lack of intelligence to me is "you know." I sense that people who rely on this phrase several times in each sentence are insecure about their opinions or information, and they feel they must elicit a positive response from their listeners to give them the courage to continue. Again, this sort of audible pause undercuts the effectiveness of communication.

It's far better simply to pause for a moment and let silence fill the gap. A strong point surrounded by silence becomes even stronger. You allow your words a little time to sink in and give the impression you feel confident about the things you've said. Of course, too much silence or slow talking can make your listener edgy and impatient and tempt him to say, "Come on, spit it out! Get it over with!" But in general, I'd choose a series of short silences to the meaningless grunts and phrases often injected into speech.

6. ECHOES ARE FOR DEEP CANYONS, NOT DEEP CONVERSATIONS. A friend of mine, a fund raiser in a big university, has followed the principle of concentrating on listening almost to a fault because he's what I'd call an "echo listener." He repeats the last few words of everything you say, and the effect can be extremely distracting. I'll say, "We're expecting that by this Monday the deal will be made," and he'll chime in, ". . . the deal will be

made." Or I'll say, "We'll meet in Pennsylvania," and he'll echo quietly, ". . . meet in Pennsylvania." After talking with him for a few minutes, I begin to watch for his lips to move as I finish up a thought, and I start concentrating more on his idiosyncrasy than on the conversation.

I'm sure he wasn't even aware of what he was doing, and the tendency to repeat things was probably just a desire to keep his entire attention on me and fix everything I said precisely in his mind. But finally, I decided that, as a friend, I had to do something to let him know how annoying this trait was. So I waited for him to repeat something, and then I said, "What? What was that?"

He hesitated, then asked, "Did I say something?"

"You said exactly what I said," I replied. "For a moment there, I thought I was repeating myself."

"I didn't realize I was saying anything out loud."

"Yes, you do that, and frankly, it gets to be irritating. Nobody likes to have what he's said repeated over and over."

I got this point across with a twinkle in my eye so that he would know that I wasn't angry at him, but rather that I was half joking at the same time I was making a serious point. I've found that kidding a person gently about his annoying trait—or at least telling him about it with a smile—is the best way to get the message across.

7. DON'T BECOME A SENTENCE-FINISHER. If you have strong opinions about a subject or think quickly about most things, you may often leap into the middle of another person's discourse and begin finishing sentences for him. This is one of the worst habits you can fall into

and may destroy a meaningful conversation because the other person begins to feel pressured to get his thoughts out before you interrupt. I have the problem myself, especially when I'm talking with a slow and deliberate speaker. Because I've been talking at a high rate of speed all my life and have heard nearly every approach to conversation there is, I can frequently predict what a person is going to say when he's halfway through a sentence— just because the sentence structure indicates to me what's coming next.

Arthur Godfrey is one of the best interviewers around, but his style of speech is much slower and more deliberate than mine. Occasionally, when we'd get together for a chat, I'd get so impatient at his pace that I'd think I was going out of my mind waiting for him to wind up a thought. "You're . . . having . . . fun . . . in the mountains," he would say, and it was all I could do to restrain myself from taking over his part of the conversation as well as my own. But I was usually glad I exercised some self-control because frequently I found that with intelligent people like Arthur, I couldn't predict the precise point he was going to make. Sometimes when I did finish a sentence, he'd have to say patiently, "No Art, that's not it; this is what I was going to say. . . ."

It's selfish and discourteous to have your say about a subject and then keep hopping back on the stage to help your companion get his points across. Frequently, you'll be more of a hindrance than a help, so let the other guy have his time in the spotlight, and wait your turn for a second opportunity to expand upon or rebut what he's been saying.

8. LEARN HOW TO GET YOUR FOOT OUT OF YOUR MOUTH.

Everyone commits faux pas periodically, but there are a number of ways to defuse a situation so that you don't hurt someone's feelings.

If I'm on a stage giving a talk, for example, and I suddenly sense I've struck a raw nerve because the atmosphere in the auditorium becomes noticeably chillier, I confront the situation directly. If I'm aware than something I said had the wrong effect, I admit it and apologize, "Actually, I didn't mean that the way it sounded, and I hope I didn't hurt anyone's feelings."

Many times when I've been on stage, poised to introduce someone who was late arriving, I'd just say to the audience, "I might as well tell you right now, for the next few minutes you're going to hear a jumble of ideas and stream of consciousness from Art Linkletter's personal philosophy because our guest hasn't shown up yet, and I'm not prepared to deliver his speech." Or, "Ladies and gentlemen, one of those things you dream about in nightmares has just happened to me. In this carefully prepared talk I've been giving you, I've just turned the page and found there's no page 8. So here is what I might have said to you if I had my notes in front of me. . . ."

I remember another time I let the sharp-edged, unkind side of my nature get the better of me when I told a man at a party, "You see that woman over there? Have you ever seen an uglier-looking dame in your life?"

"That's my wife," he replied.

"No, no, I don't mean your wife—I know who she is," I said, my mind searching wildly for an escape hatch. "It's the woman next to her."

"That's my mother."

By that time, I knew the jig was up. "You can do what

you want with me," I said with a weak smile. "Where do you want to hit me? Take your best shot."

I always try to squeeze gracefully out of a tight situation, but when there's no hope of redeeming myself, I imitate the defeated dog: He bites and scratches until he's at the end of his rope; then he rolls over and puts his feet up to show it's all over and he's ready to surrender.

9. MAKE POOR CONVERSATIONALISTS YOUR PERSONAL PROJECT. Let me make a personal confession: Because I put such a high premium on stimulating conversation, I sometimes lapse into what I call "ability snobbishness." It's a character flaw which I'm keenly aware of and which I'm constantly trying to correct. I size up a person rather quickly when I first meet him and either immediately develop a respect for his ability to think and talk, or relegate him to a position of inferiority just as quickly. If I rate him below five on a scale of ten, it's difficult for me to be courteous, so I have to be very careful and look for other ways to relate effectively to those who are not such scintillating conversationalists.

One technique I've used to overcome this problem is to assume at the outset that the person who hasn't particularly impressed me is nevertheless brighter than I am at something. The problem is to find out what that something is, so I make the poor speaker my personal project for the evening. I probe around, ask questions about his background, his opinions, his career aspirations. Inevitably, if I try hard enough, we'll reach some common ground for an interesting discussion, or, more often, I'll learn something I'd never have known if I hadn't put out a little effort to get to know the person better.

At one point, I went even further. I suffered through

an excruciatingly boring dinner party one evening because I got stuck with a guy who preferred to stare at me and respond in one-word answers to my questions. So I decided when I got home to put together an all-American team of the worst conversationalists in Los Angeles, with an individual for every position in the line and backfield. Then I resolved to penetrate that line of awful talkers and score by figuring out how each one of them could be enticed into conversation.

It was a fascinating exercise and one which sharpened my own talking skills and sensitivities. I discovered some people were just shy and would loosen up after I gave them a few minutes to warm up to me. Others had one-track interests and were simply incapable of talking about anything but their narrow fields of knowledge. With these folks, I discarded any of the usual preliminaries: "How's your family?" or "Did you read about the latest peace moves in the Mideast?" and so forth, and went right to their consuming passion. If they thought about nothing but subcontracting buildings, that's what we discussed. If their "hot button" was baseball, I immediately pressed it by asking a question about the latest trade involving the Angels. I decided not to try to swim upstream talking about ballet with someone who is insane about chess. And by sticking to the topics that interested the other person rather than me, I learned a great deal about subjects I had completely ignored.

Take a few moments now to think on paper about the various people you run into in your social circle. Divide them into good conversationalists and bad conversationalists. Then, beside each good talker, jot down the things you feel make him or her successful. Next to each bad conversationalist, write down a few ideas about how you can draw him out more—such as exploring in more depth topics that particularly interest him.

To find a mutually satisfying topic to discuss with bad conversationalists, I often use this sequence of questions to learn more about the person:

Ask about his career and try to find a pet project that he's deeply involved in. Often, if you try hard enough, you'll stay on this subject for the rest of the evening.

Ask about his or her family. If your "project" for the evening has children, you might introduce a social issue: "It's really hard to bring up kids these days, don't you think?" Or, "What activities can you find to do with your children in this city?"

Finally, move into hobbies or avocations. If the person is deeply involved in church work, for example, ask what he thinks about ordaining women as ministers.

Whatever sequence you use, you should have a plan in mind before you encounter the bad talker so that you can keep moving forward with your questions until you finally hit the right topic. One friend of mine said: "Oh, the most terrible thing happened to me the other night. I met this person at a cocktail party before dinner and found we had to sit together at the dinner. But we had already talked about everything we could think of at the cocktail party!" That, to me, reflects poor conversational planning and a little laziness too. It's as though this individual had a tank of talking fuel at the beginning of the evening and then had to apportion it through both parties but used it up too soon and had nothing to fly on. Your string of conversational strategies will become endless if you just take a little time to think through what questions you're going to ask when you encounter that all-American line of bad conversationalists in your social circle.

10. BE PREPARED TO SPEAK AT MOST SOCIAL GATHERINGS. This point may seem an unnecessary imposition, especially if you've never been asked to deliver an impromptu address at a party, dinner, or other meeting. But one of these days, someone will call on you, and if you're ready, you can take a giant leap forward in your drive to be a successful person.

I never go to a dinner party, no matter how informal, without thinking of something I could say to the group. I'll never forget one dinner party I attended at the White House while Richard Nixon was President. Prince Charles was guest of honor, and there were four former secretaries of state who had been deeply involved with Great Britain, as well as many other present and former high government officials.

I sat next to Jock Whitney, a former ambassador to Great Britain; Bob Hope sat on his other side. The speeches that evening went more quickly than I had expected. President Nixon made a few introductions, said some complimentary things about Prince Charles, and then the evening was over. As we were getting ready to leave, I leaned over to Hope and said, "Tell me the truth, Bob, did you have some material ready in case they called on you?"

"Yes, I was ready. How did you know?" he replied.

"Because I was ready too," I said. "I'm loaded with stuff I'll never use anywhere else."

Then Jock Whitney looked at us with a surprised expression and said, "Me too! I woke up with a start last night because I've been Ambassador to England, and I couldn't get back to sleep; I was thinking so hard about some opening remarks."

Then we looked across the table and noticed Bebe Rebozo sitting there. "How about you?" I asked him.

"I'm his friend because I never say anything," Rebozo replied.

He may have been the only exception in that audience! Bob Hope and I felt compelled to spend time before this dinner preparing for a possible talk before that high-powered group. If we, as professional speakers, were concerned about getting ready, how much more imperative it is for those with less experience to organize their thoughts for a possible impromptu presentation. A large part of success depends on the image you convey at social and business gatherings, and if you stammer and ramble and fall on your face before your superiors, your image and potential for success have to suffer.

This need to be prepared also applies in situations where you're meeting people for informal social conversations or sales presentations. An old trick among salespeople who are about to call on a client for a big pitch is to get a copy of one of the *Who's Who* volumes or some other source to learn the potential buyer's activities. Then the salesperson can do background research into the buyer's interests and have a conversation peg to establish some sort of relationship with him before getting into the meat of the sales talk. Of course, preparation means *thorough* preparation and not just a superficial skimming of his background, which may be a waste of time if you miss some key point. I'm reminded of one salesman who learned his prospective client was a fisherman, so he went to a local sporting goods store and picked up a half dozen books on deep sea fishing. When he finally walked in to meet his client, the salesman immediately embarked on a fishing discussion. "I understand you like to fish," he said. "I was amazed the other day when I read that the biggest swordfish ever caught off our shores was 300 pounds."

"I don't know. I'm not really into that sort of thing," the other man said.

"What do you mean?"

"I'm a trout fisherman. I specialize in dry fly outings in the Adirondacks."

The idea of getting prepared was fine, but this salesman's efforts were wasted because he had stopped short of doing an adequate job of background research.

11. BE CAREFUL WITH JOKES OR THE JOKE MAY BE ON YOU. Most people can't tell jokes effectively, but if you want to try, the absolute rule is the shorter the joke, the better. Every second that ticks by is time you're investing on behalf of your audience, and the longer your story, the bigger and funnier your punch line must be.

I only know one or two people who can successfully draw a story out for fifteen or twenty minutes, and Danny Thomas is one of them. He can embroider his anecdotes so effectively and make so many funny little asides that you really don't care about the final punch line.

There are two basic ways to be funny: First of all, any bit of humor is funnier if it arises out of an ad lib. For example, I heard one speaker respond to a loud crash at a dinner party that resulted from a waiter's dropping a bunch of plates. He turned around and said: "We've got to have that termite man out. Those beasts are going crazy again!" Now this remark may not seem so humorus out of context, but when it arose out of the situation, the audience recognized it as a spontaneous, witty response to an embarrassing situation, and they roared.

The second way to be funny is to tell a prepared joke, and for inexperienced jokesters, here's some advice George Burns gave me many years ago. He said: "If you want to tell a joke and you're not an established comedian, Art"—and I wasn't at the time—"don't take the risk of exposing yourself directly to the audience. Do it this way: 'I was talking to Jack Benny backstage, and he told me a story you can't believe. . . .' You tell the story, and you have the authority of Jack Benny transferred to you. If it doesn't go over, it's his fault, not yours."

12. UNDISCIPLINED TALK MEANS AN UNDISCIPLINED MIND. A lot of garbage is expected in any informal conversation because many times you find yourself thinking out loud, especially in a brainstorming session. But when you're in a business situation, such as a sales presentation or job interview, it's important to keep to the point. People who speak in a stream-of-consciousness fashion alienate their listeners and severely hinder their chances for success.

The worst examples of this kind of speech can be found on some of the morning talk shows. I remember one host saying to a call-in listener, "Hello, this is Joe, your Morning Milkman. What have you got to say?"

"Well, Joe, Frieda in East Lake says you were talking about problems with door-to-door salesmen, when one comes to your house . . . oh, we've got a house built in 1922—you've seen that kind of house with the little brown shutters and fake Spanish architecture . . . we bought it, of course, not because of the architecture but because it was a terrific buy . . . we had this chance—

actually it wasn't a chance, it was my uncle Ed . . . he lived there for years until his death . . . it was one of those rare diseases you don't find once in a thousand times, but he happened to be working in an asbestos factory . . . I think they ought to do something about those laws letting people work without proper safety precautions. . . ."

Someone like this doesn't know what he's thinking or saying. He keeps changing directions, overqualifying everything he says. And the result is a mishmash of words that bores the listener and gives the impression the speaker doesn't know how to think constructively.

Sometimes a truly intelligent person who talks this way doesn't actually know the poor impact he's making, and if I know him well enough, I'll try to get the message across with a little humor. I'm known as a kidder and jokester, so I can get away with saying things more serious people can't. If I were hosting that talk show, I might say: "Hold it! I don't want to know about the house! I know it's a fascinating house, but what do you think about those traveling salesmen?" Then each time he strayed from the point, I'd bring him back with a jocular, "Hold on now!" or "What direction are you heading in now?"—always with a smile or twinkle in my eye, of course.

If you're good enough, you might even try using this "diarrhea of the mouth" approach yourself. Just ramble on, exaggerating each detour, until he recognizes what you're doing. Then sit down and have a serious talk with him about his problem. In any case, though, you shouldn't simply make fun of him, or you'll lose a friend. The humor should be employed in private and should always be coupled with concerned discussion of how you want to help him get rid of his annoying habit.

Sometimes your efforts to get him to change his ways are futile, and it may be necessary to extricate yourself from a conversation with him so that you can meet someone else. One way I do this is to say, "Excuse me, your story is absolutely fascinating—but I've *got* to go to the bathroom!" Once, when I was on the phone with a long-winded woman, I said, "Jane, I want to interrupt to tell you something, but I don't want you to get frightened."

"What?" she said, startled at the suddenly urgent tone in my voice.

"The house has been on fire for about five minutes, and I've either got to call the fire department or go put it out!"

I'm sure she still wonders if the house was really on fire, or if I had to go to the bathroom and was trying to get the point across euphemistically. But whatever went through her mind, I managed to get off the phone.

13. LEARN THE PROPER PLACE FOR PLEASANTRIES. It's important to develop a sensitivity to what an employer or prospective client expects in a discussion so that you'll know what conversational style to use. Some executives want everything to be completely businesslike, getting right to the point at once and no embellishments. Others like a few pleasantries mixed in with business to relieve some of the tension of direct negotiations.

In my own case, I use either approach, depending on the individual I'm talking with, the nature of the business, or how busy my own schedule is. An insurance man came to my office once and emphasized to one of my assistants, "I'd like to talk to Linkletter about some insurance, but all I want is sixty seconds. If you'll just give me sixty seconds, that's all I ask."

He made such a big thing out of the sixty seconds that I decided to give him an audience, even though I had no particular desire to buy any more insurance. When he arrived for his appointment, I took a stopwatch out of my drawer and put it on my desk.

"Let's get acquainted," he said after we shook hands. "I'd like to tell you about how I found you. . . ." He went on to explain to me how the kinds of work he and I were in complemented each other, told a couple of little jokes, and in general was quite pleasant.

But at the end of the sixty seconds, I pointed to the watch and said, "Goodbye."

"But my sixty seconds hasn't started yet!" he protested.

"It started when you came in. You didn't say sixty seconds after we'd spent an hour getting acquainted. Goodbye."

"But . . ."

"Goodbye," I said, and ushered him toward the door.

Now, this may seem like a rough way to treat somebody, but I was extremely busy at the time, and he had been informed of that fact by my assistant. Our meeting was purely business and friendship had nothing to do with it, but he hadn't been sensitive enough to recognize that fact.

In situations where speed is less imperative or the nature of the meeting is such that you want to decide whether to establish a long-term relationship with another businessman, then you need more leeway to get acquainted. The best approach in this type of meeting is to do your homework, find out what the other guy likes, and steer the get-acquainted phase of your discussion around to those topics.

14. GET INTERESTED IN OBNOXIOUS PEOPLE. I don't believe that Will Rogers ever said or even believed that he had "never met a man I didn't like." That's one of those old saws that's ridiculous because you all meet people you don't like for one reason or another. People sometimes come up to me and say, "Gee, you like everybody, don't you?"

And I reply: "No, I don't like everybody. I'm repulsed by some people. But if I could paraphrase Will Rogers, I might say, 'I never met a man I wasn't *interested* in.' "

I'm sometimes interested in and fascinated by people because they're so incredibly unlikable. I'll ask myself what could possibly have happened to make that man or woman so utterly repulsive. I find I'm drawn into conversations with some people just to satisfy my curiosity about what makes them tick.

The same attitude applies when you're trying to sell something to a particularly hostile or obnoxious person. The fascinating thing about selling is that so much of it is an art based on the fact that every human being is unique and has to be influenced differently from every other human being. There has never been another person like you or me in the entire history of the world, and there never will be such a person again. Not only that, you're different each day, like a river that flows and changes with every foot of shoreline. So when you're trying to sell something to somebody, you have to realize that the person you're facing has to be appealed to on an individual basis. It's true that people can be classified very roughly into categories: aggressive, passive, friendly, haughty, and so on. But when you try to convince someone to have confidence in what you're saying, you have to relate to him as a unique individual. Some of the best sales can be made to people who initially seem hostile, but after several minutes of conversation, emerge as fascinating and stimulating companions.

15. AVOID OUTSIDE INTERRUPTIONS, LIKE TELEPHONES. When you're involved in a business meeting, one of the most discourteous things you can do is maintain an "open telephone." In other words, you answer your phone calls at the same time you're trying to keep some continuity in your discussions in the office.

I consider such a practice to be a personal affront, and I've actually taken some businessmen to task on the subject. One time I went to a man's office for a meeting, sat down, and the phone rang constantly during the first several minutes of our session together. He would talk on the phone for a minute or two, then we would talk for a few minutes or even seconds, and the cycle would begin anew when the next call came through.

Finally, completely exasperated, I said: "What I ought to do is leave and go out and call you so we can finish this discussion without any interruptions! Think about this situation for a minute from my point of view. I left my office and came down here for what I regarded as an important discussion. But instead, some guy who has an active finger can dial your number and get your whole attention. The people who phone you have priority over your time, but I don't."

He was extremely apologetic and seemed embarrassed, but that suited me fine because he told his secretary to hold his calls.

I've found this checklist helpful in reminding me of the most important factors in powerful speaking and conversation, and I encourage you to glance over these points again right now. Also, skim them occasionally when you're preparing for an important business meeting or social event. Good speaking, whether before an audience of thousands or in an intimate encounter with one other person, requires concentration and practice.

CHAPTER 12

Some Tips on Negotiating

In many fields of business, success comes primarily through the ability to negotiate effectively. Many of the talk power principles discussed in the last chapter apply in negotiating, but there are also some other, special skills that the good negotiator must develop, and that's what I'd like to examine now.

The first rule in negotiating successfully for an employment contract, client account, or any other business arrangement is that you must have a *definite goal in mind* before you ever begin any horse trading. Before you enter a meeting, write down precisely what it is you want to accomplish, including the highest price you're willing to pay for goods or services, or the lowest you're willing to receive if you're on the seller's side of the bargaining table. If there are nonmonetary issues, write these down and decide ahead of time how much you're willing to compromise.

After you've put your thoughts on paper, you must next decide whether you should make the first offer in the negotiations, or whether the first step should be left up to the other side. The approach you take will depend on the kind of deal that's involved and also on the amount of information that's available to help you make your decision. When the value of my services as a master of ceremonies at a banquet is involved, I always try to do some preliminary research about the financial situation of the organization I'll be working for. I learn ahead of time how many people are expected to attend, the charge per person, and the cost of the dinner, including the rest of the program that evening. I then try to figure out what the profit will be, and finally, I give serious consideration to the purpose of the event, to see if it's the kind of thing I'll support for less money if necessary.

After gathering all this information, I may conclude that this group can't afford my top fee of $10,000 because they simply won't bring in enough people to pay out that kind of money. In addition, if the purpose of the event is charitable, that would be another factor that might lead me to settle for a smaller sum.

Here's the way my negotiations might proceed in this situation:

"I usually get $10,000 for a job like this," I tell the organizer, "but you've indicated that you can't pay that much. Still, I'm interested in this event because you're promoting a cause I believe in, and besides, you're going to be holding this meeting at Niagara Falls, and I've never been there. What can you afford to pay me?"

"I think we can give you $7500," he replies.

And I say, "That's fine, and I assume you'll pick up all my first class expenses, including hotels and plane fares."

In this case, I let him know what ballpark we are playing in by stating my top fee of $10,000, but I also tell him I am willing to compromise and then toss the initiative back to him. My prior research had shown me in general terms what he could afford, so his response of $7500 was no surprise. Finally, I always try to have a "clincher," a counteroffer designed to put me in a slightly better position and yet one that's sufficiently conservative to warrant closing the deal without a lot of extra discussion. In this negotiation, my request for expenses serves as the clincher.

Although I took the lead in this particular deal, sometimes I prefer to remain passive and let the other guy take the initiative because I don't have enough facts at hand to make an intelligent offer. For example, if someone approaches me for a commercial TV deal with a national sponsor, I have to say, "What do you have in mind?" because the price depends on frequency, network size, length of the contract, etc. Generally, the more you know about the other person's business, the more aggressive you should be about setting the price.

Whether you're passive or aggressive, however, there are some tips you should keep in mind to put yourself in the most advantageous position:

1. ESTABLISH A POINT OF PERSONAL IDENTIFICATION WITH THE PERSON REPRESENTING THE OTHER SIDE. Just as I suggested increasing your talk power, do some background research on the personal background of the other fellow, and prepare some conversation openers to start a friendship with him. If you find his grandfather comes from the same part of the country as your grandfather, that fact may have nothing to do directly with your deal. But at least you may be able to say: "I bet we're going to do a considerable amount of horse trading today because the blood of a horse trader from Arkansas flows in my veins, and I heard from somebody you have the same kind of blood from your grandfather, who used to own

a ranch in Texas. We just may end up trading each other two dead horses!"

Or you might begin by saying: "When I was in Atlanta last year, I ran into a guy who had made one of the most serious mistakes of his life. He said he agreed to sit in with you for a friendly game of poker, and he hasn't paid for his new pants and shirt yet!" By such remarks, you flatter the guy by acknowledging his ability to take risks successfully and also forge a small bond that may later flower into a fruitful business relationship.

2. THE QUESTION OF WHETHER TO USE AN AGENT IS A HIGHLY PERSONAL MATTER. It depends as much on your personality as on what you hope to get out of the bargaining sessions. I've never had an agent, though I've worked with them when they bring deals to me. Although I happen to be a fairly good negotiator, I have no doubt that I could have made half again as much money during my career had I used a tough Hollywood agent. But I've done well financially without one, and just as important, I've enjoyed doing my own negotiating. There are so many personal reasons that I get involved in different jobs—reasons that have nothing to do with money—that I know I might have lived quite a different life if I had given control of my affairs to another person.

3. ALWAYS TAKE NOTES WHILE YOU'RE DISCUSSING A DEAL. I've gotten into the habit of always taking notes conspicuously as I discuss a business arrangement so that the other parties will see what I'm doing and remember that a record of sorts is being kept. And I always keep the notes in a safe place so that I can produce them in case there is any question about what was said in the meeting.

One time I got into a business that involved installing

low voltage wiring in houses in such a way that the need for insulation and the possibility of fire problems were greatly reduced. It was a cheap, marvelous device and we did a good business, but some differences developed between me and my three partners as to how the company should develop in the future. I wanted to change some things and go for even higher profits at a greater risk, but they were happy with the safer profits they were making.

Deciding that the time had come to part ways, we set up a meeting to negotiate the arrangements under which they would buy my stock. We had dinner together, came to final terms, and then set up another meeting to draw up the final contracts with our lawyers. But as we started talking at this last session, some basic disagreement arose:

I said, "This is what the deal was," but they responded, "That wasn't the deal at all! This was the deal!"

"You must be kidding!" I retorted, but all three of them agreed that I had misunderstood the terms that we had settled on at that dinner meeting. I turned to my lawyer and sighed, "Here we go!" I could see the beginnings of a three-year lawsuit

But then one of my partners, the managing director, said: "Art, after that last meeting, I went back to my office and wrote down what we agreed on, and I put the paper in my desk. Let's go back and see what I wrote."

As we piled into our cars and went to his office, I was thinking that I would look like the jerk of the year if the position they were advocating were down in black and white. We all gathered around his desk as the director pulled the paper out, but as he read it, his face began to change.

"You're right, Art," he said.

"What do you mean?" the other two guys said.

"Look at it," the director replied, handing them the paper, and the argument was settled in my favor.

That incident has convinced me not only to take notes after an important meeting but to jot things down during the actual discussion. Between honest, honorable business people, such a record may eliminate the need for additional negotiations or court proceedings.

4. Don't drive too hard a bargain. Many businessmen consider driving an extremely hard bargain—in effect skinning the guy on the other side of the table alive—to be a very commendable practice. But actually, it's much wiser to give in on a few points if you have the leeway so that the other negotiators won't leave with a bad taste in their mouths. Most times, when you get down to the final stages of your bargaining, you've usually insured that everybody's going to do well. The question then becomes more of an ego contest, to see which person can come out a little ahead, regardless of the irreparable harm that may be done to human relationships in the process.

I love to make a deal, a fair deal in which both sides do well. I once fired an attorney who came to me after I had signed a contract because he proudly showed me how we had legally—but immorally—bested someone else. I always stand up for my rights, but I think the fact that I once had nothing makes me bend over backward now to see that the other person gets a fair shake. It's so easy to be tough when you're on top; the mark of a civilized man, though, is to put fairness above any temptation to take advantage.

This willingness to give a little, to see the other fellow's problems and point of view, is one of the reasons

I had one show on the air for nineteen and another for nearly twenty-five years. During tough times when big shows were being canceled all around us, we endured because my partner and I were always willing to bend a little in our negotiations over contract interpretations. When we were riding really high, number one across the country for years, I didn't come back to our sponsors and say, "Well, you know I'm so hot now that I don't think this is a fair contract." A deal is a deal for me, and although new contracts are always subject to new terms and clauses, the bargaining process was never a high-pressure thing for me. I never held success out as a threat to the people who had placed their faith in me in the first place. In this regard, I can't help but feel that the current fashion in show business and sports to try to squeeze every drop out of temporary rises in popularity or box-office appeal is bound to be counterproductive in the long run.

By relaxing some of the details and finer points I know I could have won over the years, I've lost a little money, but I've also made friends out of clients. And when the decision would come up a few months or years later about whom to pick for another deal, I believe I've been given preference over the guy who tried to carry the other fellow's scalp away with an excessively tough contract.

5. ALWAYS DO MORE THAN WHAT YOUR CONTRACT CALLS FOR. This point is a corollary to the previous one and has the same purpose underlying it: to leave a good taste in the other guy's mouth and provide a basis for a profitable, continuing relationship.

I still try to live by this principle when I get involved in various job responsibilities. If I'm speaking at a convention, the leaders of the group may ask, "Do you mind coming to cocktails before the speech so that you can visit with some of our top officers?" I usually do it, even though I hate cocktail parties, because I want them to feel I'm interested in them as people and not as just the source of a paycheck. I can also do a better job because I can "feel out" the mood and purpose of the group.

The same approach would apply to the person who takes a job with the understanding that office hours end at 5 P.M. It's easy to say, "I'm leaving right at 5 o'clock today even though I haven't finished this assignment, because I'm only getting paid for eight hours' work." But the person who makes a good impression on employers and who ultimately gets ahead in life is the one who puts in that extra hour and focuses on the successful completion of the task at hand, rather than on his rights under some formal work agreement.

6. SLEEP ON MAJOR DECISIONS IN NEGOTIATIONS. You may think you've nailed down a contract just the way you had planned, but it's always best to back off for at least a day, if possible, and reflect on the deal from a distance. The best terms and the most fantastic insights sometimes take on a different color in the cold light of the following morning.

I always like to say, "I have this partner or associate I'd like to have go over this before we sign any papers"— especially if the negotiations have been unusually complex. Even if you don't have a partner or seasoned associate, a good lawyer or even an objective spouse can often poke holes in an agreement or at least raise important questions you've overlooked.

Learning to influence people—through friendship networks, self-promotion, effective conversation techniques, and negotiating skills—is perhaps the most important factor in your road to success in life. But unless you can deliver the goods by doing a good job once you get people behind you, all that stress on persuasive communication may be in vain.

PART FOUR

How to Excel in Your Work

CHAPTER 13

How to Be an Idea Person

People are always coming up to me and saying, "I'm not an idea person—I'm just not very creative." This kind of negative attitude is self-defeating and will often lead to failure in life. Not only that, such a view of yourself is inherently inaccurate because *anyone* can be an idea person with a little training and practice.

It's true that some people are quicker and seem to generate more ideas than other people. And it's often impossible to analyze precisely why these creative individuals are so full of new concepts. Neil Simon, or "Doc" Simon as I've known him since he was a script writer around Hollywood years ago, is perhaps the most successful Broadway light comedy writer in history. At a dinner recently, he said: "I was asked by a college if I'd like to teach a course in creative writing, but I told them I don't know how! I create, but I just don't know how I do it, and I certainly can't teach it!"

I agree with Neil that the source of some of these great ideas is a mystery. They originate by a process that can't be explained. But you can increase your output of ideas, even if you do not reach the high-flown levels of creativity of a Neil Simon. The first step is to develop the three basic elements of idea-generating: flooding your brain with information, risking ridicule, and brainstorming with others.

The best way to *flood your brain with information* is to read everything you can get your hands on, especially those things that relate directly to your field of interest. I used to get a great number of my best ideas for the "House Party" and "People Are Funny" shows from the daily newspapers. Once I read a story about a policeman who had been fooled by a check forger. The cop was red-faced when the check bounced, and he was quoted as saying, "Gee, that guy looked so honest!"

When I noticed that item, I thought, You know, people are funny! We all think we have some divine gift which enables us to look at another person and see right into his soul. We gaze into his blue, unwavering eyes, admire his clean, pleasant face, and we know the guy is telling us the truth. We can always tell a crook—or at least that's what we believe—until we get ripped off by one of these clean-cut fellows!

So I decided to begin a series of features where a contestant would come up out of the audience and examine four photos. I'd tell him that one of the men was a notorious bank robber and ask him to pick the guy out. Or I'd line up the live "suspects" in the front row of the audience and pose the same question. Invariably the man who looked least like a bank robber would be the one, and the others, who were usually tougher-looking than most ex-cons, would be identified as the president of a local bank or corporation, or an official of the Y.M.C.A.

Other television programs have since been put on the air that use just this same technique, and they've been tremendously popular with audiences because everyone likes to get in on the guessing game. But I might never have come up with the idea if I hadn't been an avid newspaper reader.

No matter how much information you have, however, you'll never hone your idea faculties to a fine edge unless you throw out those ideas to others and *take the risk of being laughed at*. Such risk-taking takes a great deal of self-confidence, but it's absolutely essential if you hope to be a successful originator of new concepts. For example, if you're in the tire manufacturing business, you know many good tires have been developed during the past seventy years, but there's still not one that will stop a car going seventy miles per hour in ten feet. Even with all the radial construction, there's still plenty of room for improvement. So suppose the idea pops into your head to put small hooks on tires to slow down the car? Now, that sounds crazy to me, but with your engineering and scientific skill, if you sense there may be something to the notion, you should toss the idea out for examination. Some of the greatest inventions of all time started as offbeat figments of the imagination.

Finally, if you've crammed your mind with facts and been willing to take a chance on being rejected as you propose your ideas to someone, you've arrived at the third element of idea generation: *brainstorming*. Brainstorming is the process by which a group of idea people get together and discuss and refine their new concepts in an effort to arrive at a final plan which an organization can successfully put into practice. Sometimes, you can come up with an idea, refine it, and put it into practice all by yourself and make a million dollars. But more often, you must allow others to make suggestions to modify your original concept so that you can get the best product possible.

Here's the way one of my own brainstorming sessions might work: While discussing the best way to get an opening laugh for a comedy scene, somebody makes a silly suggestion that two guys ride in on a camel. Immediately, another person says: "No, that wouldn't work. The set isn't big enough, and you know what a camel does all over the floor!"

"Yeah, throw out the camel," another one agrees. "But how about a llama? That's sounds funny—it's a funny word. We could make some good jokes with a word like that—you know, he's going on the lam with a loan on a llama." Not great, perhaps, but you're on the way. . . .

After you've laid the groundwork by developing a positive approach toward information-gathering, risk-taking, and brainstorming, here are some specific techniques that will help you become an effective idea person.

First of all, find the precise approach to ideas that suits your personality best. Some people, for instance, are good at coming up with original theories—things that no one has ever thought of before. More often, though, the most impressive idea people are synthesizers—those who gather together concepts that others have found and then put them together into a new and stimulating arrangement. My close friend, Bill Lear, who was one of the greatest inventors in American history and responsible for the development of the Lear jet, once told me that he never *invented* anything in his life. Instead, he took a number of known principles and put them together in a new and different way. You can't create something from nothing—that takes special genius—but you can *im-*

prove on almost anything within your sphere of influence. It's just a matter of spending some time mulling over the "knowns" or "givens" in your business and fitting them together into a new pattern.

A second technique that should help you to generate ideas is getting into the habit of walking away from a tough problem. This may sound self-defeating, but it's not. You often get so close to a project that you lose perspective, and the best way to infuse some fresh thinking or to break a mental block is to walk around the block or go play some tennis or golf. When you return to your desk, you can resolve your problem more easily. There may even be a physiological explanation for this phenomenon. Perhaps when you get up and move around, your blood starts circulating more rapidly and that helps your brain provide a detour around the difficulty.

Another idea-generating technique that I've noticed in my professional circles is the note pad. The most creative people I know always carry one of these pads and jot down thoughts during the day as they come to mind. I do this myself, though not as much as I should. When I hear something clever or imagine something funny, I think, That's so funny I'm sure I'll never forget it, but sometimes I forget even the most fascinating morsels. Even if it's only a fragmentary reflection, jot it down so that you'll have something to jog your memory. I don't think it's an overstatement to say that the failure to be an idea person is the failure to write down significant concepts and thoughts.

A fourth technique I use in generating ideas is to concentrate on fields that I'm particularly familiar with. For instance, suppose you're thinking about trying to start your own business. Don't waste time trying to figure out how to market television sets if you know nothing about electronics or related subjects. On the other hand, if you're an avid gardener, think about starting a plant store with a special counseling booth for people with ailing houseplants; or try to develop string beans that have self-destructing strings for finicky cooks. Try also to discipline your reading and thinking so that you keep abreast of the innovative developments in your special fields of interest.

Finally, remember that ideas tend to pop up simultaneously in different people's minds. If you have a good idea, assume that someone else is also thinking about it or is about to get it. When Ralph Edwards with "Truth or Consequences" and John Guedel and I with "People Are Funny" were hot competitors on the air, we often came up with the same oddball idea. The one who happened to put it on his program first would be suspected by the other of having stolen it. Things got rather acrimonious between us sometimes; yet in retrospect, I'm sure that because we were both thinking about the same kinds of subjects, we came up with similar ideas quite independently of one another. The lesson, then, is clear: If a creative thought comes to your mind, *act on it immediately*! If you don't, someone else may beat you to it.

Because this realm of ideas is so important for your success in life, take some time now to try to apply some of the principles and techniques discussed. Think briefly over your business activities, your hobbies, or anything else that takes a good bit of your time and attention. In light of the goals you set for youself, which specific area of your activities is the most important to you? Pick your key area and think about what problems you or the other workers in your company encounter in doing a good job in this sphere. Problem areas are always a fertile field for new ideas, and the more solutions you come up with, the more you'll impress your employer or clients.

Now that you've isolated the particular aspect of your life that needs an injection of creativity, try this exercise. Write your problem as concisely as possible; then list as many ways of attacking it as you can think of. Be absurd! Let your fantasies run wild because you can always reject the solutions that clearly won't work. The idea is to get your mind working as freely and broadly as possible so that you can break free of your normal mindset and find an approach no one else has thought of. Then, when you have a good list of ideas, pick those that seem most promising and analyze them. See how many permutations of each one you can find, and by the time you're finished, you'll probably be operating on a level of high-powered thinking you've never experienced before.

Idea people are at a premium in business these days. Top executives always worry that they're gong to run out of new concepts, or that their time will be so consumed by the everyday concerns of management that they won't be able to devote adequate time to quiet thinking and creative planning. These anxieties make them want to surround themselves with imaginative individuals who can infuse new life into the old, traditional ways of tackling corporate projects. If you can convince your boss that you are a real idea person, you'll find yourself in great demand for high-level policy discussions and, inevitably, for promotions.

CHAPTER 14

The Rule of Ten

Whenever I suggest that it's necessary to work hard to achieve success, many people just tune me out. We live in a society where we expect success to come easily, and when it doesn't, we cast about for some quick, sure-fire formula to get rich with as little effort as possible.

In fact, hard, persistent effort *is* necessary if we hope to achieve anything in life. The so-called overnight success is, more often than not, a final, spectacular breakthrough after years of painstaking training and diligence. My own personal way of stating this principle is in terms of a "rule of ten": If anything is worth trying at all, it's worth trying at least ten times. Then, if you're still not succeeding on the eleventh try, reevaluate your techniques or drop the project altogether.

In selling, for example, the most successful people know that they have to make a certain number of phone calls or knock on a given number of doors to get results. It's a matter of percentages. Every good salesman will evaluate his progress by comparing the proportion of interested prospects and closings (final sales) with the total number of contacts he makes each day. A salesman has to get used to constant refusals, defeats, and negative reactions, but he learns that if he makes a certain number of calls—say thirty a day—he should expect a certain return in commissions—say, $350 a week. With that $350, he'll be able to pay his basic bills, and if he works a little harder, he'll have enough to bowl, play tennis, or make payments on that thirty-five-foot boat he dreams of sailing on weekends. It's the endurance that comes from persistence which enables him to put up with the door slammed in his face, trudge on to the next door, and summon up another smile.

This rule of ten also applies in many other areas of life. If you're applying for a job, it's silly to apply only to two or three places, especially if you're in a competitive field. I know of one young journalist who mailed about two hundred resumes to different newspapers around the country and got only two or three responses—but one of those responses resulted in a job. If he had sent out five or six applications, he might have been turned down by all, gotten discouraged, and decided to go into another field. In the direct mail field, marketing specialists often feel they're doing well if they get a 2–3 percent response from mailing hundreds of thousands of bulk mail appeals. If you take a similarly realistic attitude toward your own efforts to achieve success, you'll be much more likely to keep trying until you get a favorable response.

I've chosen the rule of ten as a general rule of thumb, but you must be realistic about the potential for success in the particular field you've chosen. Writers, for example, often have to endure many more than ten rejection slips before they place a manuscript. My friend Irving Stone, the author of such popular works as *The Agony and the Ecstasy* and *Lust for Life,* received enough rejection slips as a young writer to paper his apartment.

And there are song writers like the famous Sammy Cahn who went from publisher to publisher auditioning his songs and was thrown out of many offices before getting his first hit. Hollywood is full of stories of writers who lugged their movie scripts from one lot to the next, sometimes for years, before getting an acceptance that started them on their way. During the last ten years in my new career as a drug crusader, I have been frustrated dozens of times when young people with whom I had been working painfully for weeks, suddenly disappeared back into the drug world and left me almost tearfully disappointed. Workers in the halfway houses and drug treatment centers learn to go on after literally hundreds of failures, sometimes working with the same young person over and over again, only to lose him.

In yet another field I've learned the importance of persistence. As a broadcaster for World Vision, International, I have traveled to a dozen Third World countries taping experiences with the hungry and diseased "have-nots" who crowd around the centers where food and medicine are dispensed. An overwhelming sense of hopelessness occasionally gets to the most experienced of the Christian relief workers, but they keep on, knowing that while they are helping thousands, millions are dying around them. I visited a missionary and his wife deep in the Sahara desert who had been working with the poverty-stricken tribesmen of that Niger country. When I asked him how many converts he had made so far, he brightly replied that in three years, they had persuaded one person to listen to them read the Bible. That, my friends, is the rule of ten extended to its most improbable length!

The rule of ten, in other words, may have to become

the rule of one hundred or one thousand, depending on the kind of work you're doing. In an ordinary sales situation, however, begin to review your goals and performance if you find you are still failing, with no sign of progress, after ten tries. There might be something wrong with your presentation, for example. To determine whether or not this is the case, check with other salesmen who are pushing the same product you're working with, and see how you compare. If you find you're getting nowhere, and nine other guys are selling regularly to approximately the same kind of buyers, you know the product is all right. The problem must be in the way you're explaining the benefits of the product, or the way your sales pitch is organized, or even in the way you look. It's necessary for everyone, no matter how accomplished, to go back periodically and study the fundamentals of his trade. Just as baseball players have to work on their batting form when they hit a slump, or violinists have to practice their scales to keep their talents at a fine edge, so you too should return, on occasion, to the basics of your trade. If you find you can't understand what you're doing wrong through self-evaluation, don't hesitate to share your disappointments with a colleague. You might say, "You really had a great month, Joe, but there's something wrong with me, and I can't figure out what it is. Where do you think I'm missing the boat?"

The kind of persistence that leads to success in life may also involve the courage to dig in when something seems destined for disaster and by the force of your own dogged determination, transform a losing situation into a winner. In the early days of my own career, I was in charge of organizing a national radio program for a big world's fair, and the main speaker was Charles Kettering, the genius who invented the self-starter for General Motors and after whom the Memorial Sloan-Kettering Cancer Center in New York City is named.

When he arrived from Detroit for the program. I explained the schedule to him: "Mr. Kettering, I planned the entire program according to suggestions some of your subordinates have made. The orchestra will open briefly with our fair's theme music; you'll talk for forty-five minutes; and then we'll close with the theme."

The tycoon looked at me disapprovingly and retorted, "Nonsense—I won't talk for more than ten minutes."

"You can't do that!" I blurted out in protest, unthinkingly. I don't suppose anybody had told him he couldn't do anything he wanted to for at least twenty-five years.

He looked rather startled at first, but then he coolly replied, "Yes I can. I'll just sit down."

"I don't mean you *can't* do that," I explained. "What I mean is the whole program has been planned for you to take that much time, and we don't have anything else."

"Have your orchestra play some more music," he said.

"The program is only ten minutes away, and the musicians don't have any other arrangements. They haven't rehearsed except for this one theme. They're not like a dance band, with an entire repertoire of songs."

He was still shaking his head negatively when I turned to his wife in desperation. "Mrs. Kettering," I said, "do you like 'California Here I Come'?"

"It's a very pretty number," she smiled.

"Well, if you can't convince your husband to fill forty-five minutes, I hope you're going to enjoy seventy-five choruses of it because that's what they're going to play."

Mrs. Kettering spoke to Mr. Kettering. Mr. Kettering spoke for forty-five minutes.

Most top salesmen use the same I-won't-take-no-for-an-answer approach. Ben Feldman of East Liverpool, Ohio, generally recognized as the most successful life insurance salesman of all time, once sold nearly $85 million in life insurance in one year—and his primary secret is really no secret at all. A great believer in hard work, he worked seven days a week during much of his career and still puts in twelve-hour days. He also attributes much of his success to staying with a prospect indefinitely until a sale is made.

"When a man says, No," he explained to a writer for *The New York Times Magazine,* "quite often he isn't saying, No! He doesn't mean to say, No. He doesn't quite understand what it is you're presenting to him. Because what it is, if he understood it—he wouldn't say, No. People want to help themselves."

This statement by Feldman exudes self-confidence. He refuses to accept a rejection because he *knows* what he's selling is good for the other fellow, and he's determined to get his point across no matter how long it takes. The idea that his product may not be quite right for the prospective buyer doesn't even enter his head. Instead of letting negativism overcome him after that initial No, he continues to concentrate on the positive and searches even harder for that key to unlock the other guy's will and convince him to say Yes. And this kind of persistence works. His son, Marvin, told the *Times*: "There's one doctor in Beaver Falls whom he called on for twenty years. Then one year he bought. That's not unusual."

All this talk about seven-day weeks and persistence and

hard work may have depressed you temporarily. In fact, at this point you may even wish you had never read this chapter. But the more effort you put into a project, the more likely you are to experience a sensation that exhilarates your whole being. You may find that you're getting a new and thrilling "high" out of your job.

I know a fellow who vowed that he would never run for fun or money. He had disliked it while training for sports in school; he had hated it in the military; and he wasn't about to get involved in the jogging craze that seemed to be sweeping the nation. But then a friend of his, an exercise physiologist, talked him into doing a little roadwork as a way to increase his endurance in other areas of his life and also as a protection against heart disease. He decided to give it a try just for a week or so. . . . Now, after running several miles a day for a couple of years, he's discovered he couldn't quit for any reason. It's the highlight of his day.

Intense effort, whether physical or mental, always seems to result in a second wind which allows you to start feeling comfortable at a greater output. At first glance, then, my stress on hard work may seem like a call to masochism. But if you keep at it long enough, you'll develop the work habit, and the reward will be a deep sense of satisfaction from your accomplishments.

CHAPTER 15

How to Appear Knowledgeable

How many times have you heard someone say, in referring to an acquaintance, "He's really bright," or "She's really well educated, don't you think?"

In fact, the person in question may be no smarter than you are, but he or she may have the ability to convey the *appearance* of exceptional intelligence. And in a society which is as concerned with "image" as ours, the appearance of a highly trained intellect may be as important as the intellect itself.

It's important to devote some time to doing public relations for your abilities because your business associates and clients can evaluate you only on the basis of the information you provide them. If you hide your talents, your boss will have little on which to base a promotion or raise.

Here are some simple steps to help you put your knowledge and intelligence in the spotlight:

1. DON'T TRUST YOUR MEMORY. Some people have a remarkable memory for names, jokes, all sorts of factual information, but I don't trust my memory for anything. I write down anything that I consider important so that I can be certain I'll have it available when I need it. If

you need current information on several fields, it's also helpful to keep files of clippings or note cards so you can go right to the subject matter you need.

I never speak from notes during the scores of speeches I give each year, but I always pull out notes or clippings I've collected to review certain ideas and jokes before I go on stage. I also find it helpful to keep a working library with a small number of books that have impressed me during my recent reading. Underlining these key books in red and then reviewing them periodically can also put a wealth of facts and concepts at your fingertips without making you feel you have to commit everything to memory.

2. READ PERIODICALS REGULARLY AND SELECTIVELY. You're inundated with information these days—Niagaras of printed, verbal, and visual material that flood your consciousness. Because of the volume of this information, it's necessary to pick and choose the specific newspapers and magazines that you feel will provide you with the most useful information. Then skim the table of contents of each thoroughly before you start reading, and flag any articles that particularly interest you. If there's an item you want to save for your files, rip it out immediately, even before you read it, though you may want to leave it inserted in the magazine in case someone else in the family hasn't seen the publication yet. By clipping immediately, you avoid the time-wasting process of thumbing back through the same publication days or even weeks later to find the article.

The average person should read at least one newspaper a day, two or three magazines a week, and one good fiction or nonfiction book every couple of months. This amount of reading strikes me as the minimum to keep you well enough informed to discuss subjects of current interest with business acquaintances and should also give you a regular source of information for ideas necessary to the most successful execution of your work.

3. ANTICIPATE QUESTIONS FROM BUSINESS COLLEAGUES. All the reading in the world won't help you much, though, unless you do it critically. As you read through the newspapers and magazines you've chosen, ask yourself, How can I apply this to my job? Or, What's my opinion of what the writer is saying here? Through this method, you'll begin to prepare yourself to answer questions and challenges from other business associates.

When you know you'll be involved in a meeting on a particular subject, you can do even more specific preparation. Set aside about half an hour the night before the meeting, and list the subjects you expect to be discussed. Then jot down specific questions you think are likely to be posed by key persons attending the meeting. You'll be surprised how close you can come to anticipating who will talk about what, and by using your files and underlined cards in the time you have before the meeting starts, you'll find you can put yourself in an extremely strong position to participate intelligently in the discussion. Anticipating topics in this way can convey to your superiors that you're more alert and responsive to conversational gambits than the next guy. And the brighter you look in these policy and planning sessions, the more likely it is that you'll be tapped for higher job responsibilities and raises.

4. THROW OUT OBSOLETE FILES AND BOOKS. This point may seem self-evident, but so few people are willing to do it! You tend to regard written materials as somehow holy, and the idea of destroying them or giving them away

is abhorrent. But because you collect so much information, it's absolutely essential, both for efficient organization of your files and simply to make room for new items, to get rid of the old ones. Otherwise, you'll find you're becoming an informational pack rat who has such a collection of notes and clips and books that you can't retrieve the ones you need when the occasion arrives.

Although I have no hesitation about throwing away outdated written matter, I can sympathize with those who do procastinate, because I have my own pet pack rat syndrome: I never want to discard old suits. I've convinced myself that some day those fashion experts will bring back narrow pants and ties, and I'll have them there in my closet. Of course, I'm fooling myself because when the fashions do change, the designers will cleverly mix the new combinations so that my clothes will always be just far enough out of style to look tacky if I try to wear them again.

Old information carries the same basic flaw. The longer you hold it, the more outdated it becomes, and if you try to rely on favorite statistics or arguments that were written five years ago, you may find yourself red-faced when another colleague springs new concepts or figures on you. Some books are certainly classics, and certain notes or thoughts you jotted down several years ago may still be valid. But be ruthless in identifying the obsolete information in your office and discarding it (or donating it to a thrift shop for a tax deduction—old books are particularly useful for this purpose). Then you'll have moved a long way toward keeping both your office and your mind clear for the new facts and concepts that bombard you each day.

5. AVOID BECOMING POMPOUS WITH YOUR KNOWLEDGE.

Even if you succeed in assimilating and using information so as to seem the smartest person in your set, you'll fail in your ultimate purpose of becoming successful if you alienate people with arrogance. I know a number of people who are basically good-hearted, but they sport a veneer of erudition that's so threatening or obnoxious that most other people don't like to be around them. To be successful in life, the most important personality characteristic is the ability to relate to others. If your knowledge gets in the way of these relationships, it makes no difference how many facts you have at your fingertips—you'll still wind up a loser.

Getting across the appearance of being knowledgeable without seeming pompous or pedantic is an art that takes practice and sensitivity, but if you take time to notice how your words are being received by others, you'll find you can make fast progress toward your goal. For example, I've found that expressing enthusiasm for a particular subject is one of the most effective approaches to avoid seeming like a would-be egghead or instructor. I might say: "Did you know scientists are claiming there are two theories about the origin of the universe, and some physicists actually say one of the theories will support the account of creation in Genesis and the other won't? Now, I'm no scientist, but I found that notion to be fascinating. What do you think?"

By using this technique, you can convey the breadth of your reading through a sense of wonder at new knowledge you've acquired without making the other person think you regard yourself as superior.

In setting forth these five steps, I don't want to give the impression that I believe acquiring knowledge should have only a practical, work-oriented dimension to it. On the contrary, one of the major reasons I try to accumulate a large cross-section of knowledge is just plain, old-fashioned pleasure. I'm sure there must be violinists who would be happy playing a concerto on a deserted island just because they like what they're doing. I feel somewhat the same way about reading. I gobble up books and magazines by the score, not because I always expect to get something useful out of them, but simply because reading is an activity I love. Even when you're reading for pleasure, there's a subtle growth and transformation that takes place in your personality. As you increase your understanding of current facts and concepts, you develop not merely an appearance of being knowledgeable, but an actual increase in the level of your education and in your understanding and appreciation of your job and life in general.

CHAPTER 16

Stretch for Success

No matter how carefully you prepare for a job or how much knowledge you acquire, you can never be completely certain that you're ready to move up to the next rung on the career ladder. There's always an element of risk involved. When you move up to that higher position, you'll find that you will inevitably make mistakes. You may even fail.

This fear of the unknown, of the inherent risks involved in upward occupational mobility, makes many people frightened to accept new experiences. But if you expect to succeed in a big way, you have to overcome these fears and regard each challenge as an exciting adventure.

There are many aphorisms that have been developed to express this truth about the necessity of risk-taking: "You must reach beyond your grasp," or "You must aim above the target to hit the bull's-eye." However you want to express it, they all reflect a common truth: that it's essential to set your sights sufficiently high so that your goal may seem above your abilities. If you shoot any lower, you'll find yourself in a job that will soon bore you, rather than provide you with a chance to extend yourself and grow.

When I was in San Diego State College studying to be an English teacher, I wrote a weekly humor column in our school paper. One day, a committee headed by a young woman approached me, and the spokesman said, "We think you have a good batting average with your jokes, so we've nominated you to write a musical comedy for the school this year."

I thought the suggestion was a comedy in itself. "I've never written a musical comedy," I replied, "and I don't believe I've ever even seen one."

But she and her colleagues insisted I could do it. All I had to do was think up a corny plot and inject some songs and jokes that would be as funny as the quips in my humor columns. "We'll need it in about two months, and I know it'll be a lot of fun for you," she said.

I wasn't so certain, but I accepted anyhow. I knew there was a fair chance that I would fall flat on my face, but I decided to take the risk and stretch my talents. I've been grateful for that decision ever since. Somehow I finished the play, and it was a success. But even more important, the manager of the local radio station was in the audience and liked what he saw. He called the school the next day and asked, "Who wrote the script for the play?" Soon the telephone rang in the cafeteria kitchen where I was serving soup.

"I'm looking for creative young guys who might fit into a new program I'm starting, and I wonder if you'd be interested in a job?" he asked.

I accepted and thus began my career in radio.

There have been other occasions when I applied for

jobs that were far beyond my capabilities, but a certain degree of ingenuity and *chutzpah* saw me through to a successful conclusion. When I was a kid bumming around the country during the Depression, I was sometimes desperately in need of a job just to have money for food. At one of these low points, I noticed a sign on a building saying an electric arc welder was needed, so I went right in and said, "I'm an electric arc welder," even though I didn't have the slightest notion what the job entailed.

But the man in the personnel office fortunately didn't ask any probing questions. He just had me fill out a card and sent me several buildings down the street to see the foreman on the project. I handed my card to the foreman, and he asked, "You're an electric arc welder, are you?"

"No," I replied.

"What do you mean, no?"

"I haven't got the faintest idea what an electric arc welder does," I replied.

"Well, what the hell are you doing down here then?" he said.

"Without this card, I couldn't even have gotten in here to see you," I replied honestly. "But here I am, a thousand miles away from home, without a quarter, and I think I'm smart enough to fit into something in your shop. Isn't there anything here I could work at?"

He thought for a moment, amused by my boldness, and then replied, "Maybe you can be a grinder."

"What's that?"

He explained that the job entailed a minimum of skill. All I had to do was to man a whirling disk of sandpaper to grind off the beads on the steel left by the arc welder. In any case, I got the job and made enough to fill my belly until I was ready, a few weeks later, to hop the next train out of town.

Sometimes when you try for a job that's above your abilities, you may find you get it, and then you have to do some fast thinking and quick studying to learn new skills to pull yourself up to the required level. I know of one man who applied for and got a job as an accountant for a large auto company, but his accounting skills were far inferior to what the job required. He was an ingenious fellow, however, and he managed to develop a highly effective method of learning on the job. When his superior would call him in for a discussion about some fine point of accounting and this young man realized he didn't know the answer, he would excuse himself to make a run for the bathroom. Then he would detour to his office, get his accounting manual, look up the answer to the question while he was in the rest room, and return to give his superior a detailed solution to the problem.

In my own case, I took a job in New York City as secretary to a doctor on Park Avenue. I may have been a champion typist when I was in high school, but I didn't know a thing about shorthand, and that was one of the requirements of the job. I thought I could come up with an effective system of taking dictation in the few days before I embarked on this job, but my amateurish system broke down completely the first time it was put to the test. So I went back to my desk with bits and pieces of the letter the doctor wanted written, and I filled in the rest out of my own words.

"Did I say that?" he wondered, looking at some of my phrasing.

"Yes, I believe you did," I replied, "although I may have misheard a word or two."

"Actually, it sounds better than I usually do," he grinned, "so keep up the original writing."

And so we reached an accommodation for future correspondence in which I typed his letters using half his words and half mine.

All this may sound daring, and it *can* be an adventure to embark on responsibilities that make you stretch your levels of performance to their outer limits. It takes a great deal of self-confidence and positive thinking to take these leaps upward to tasks you may feel you're not quite ready for. But there are certain limits to this stretching for success. I would never take a job which I knew was so far above my abilities that I might hurt the other person's business by my incompetence. In my job at the doctor's office, I was betting that I could be so helpful with my typing and general organizational tasks that the problem with the shorthand would pale into insignificance. But I would never hold myself out as a brain surgeon and start wielding a scalpel just for the excitement of the experience.

There's a constant conflict between thinking big and being coldly realistic about your capabilities, and rather than sell yourself short, it's better to err, if you must, on the positive, expansive side. If you find yourself in a position that seems to be overtaxing your skills, don't be too quick to feel it was a mistake. You have to try things that may be slightly above your comfort quotient for a time. But if you keep working and learning and improving—and it may take a year or more to achieve a more comfortable state of mind—you'll find you're light years ahead of where you would have been if you had been more conservative and set your sights for an easier mark. No matter how tough the job seems at the time, you fail only when you say "I quit," as the old saying goes. And as long as you keep trying, you haven't failed. You just haven't succeeded yet.

CHAPTER 17

How to Multiply Yourself

No successful persons reaches the top by himself. Everyone needs friends to support and advise him.

A large part of genuine self-confidence is the ability to put trust in others. No one, no matter how brilliant, can do everything by himself, and if you try to operate in isolation, you're more likely to fall flat on your face. Or, as the Book of Proverbs puts it, "Without counsel plans go wrong, but with many advisers they succeed." (Prov. 15:22.)

When you seek advice from another, you'll find that you often have gained a valuable ally. Most people are motivated by pride as much as by money, and if they have made suggestions and you've used them, they will want to see your project succeed, for they know a failure will reflect on them as well as on you.

Now, having assumed that associates are essential to your success, let's examine how you can do the most effective job of staffing your office so that you can multiply your chances of achieving success. If you're a small businessman, the first question is whether the time is right for you to hire anyone. Or if you think you definitely need somebody, should you try to get someone on a part-time basis.

There's always a temptation, when you sit down to calculate what a secretary or assistant will cost you, to decide to pocket the money yourself and do without the extra help. But in taking this approach, you may be putting an arbitrary ceiling on your success potential. The old adage that you have to spend money to make money applies to hiring employees as much as it does to investing capital in your plant. If you're uncertain about hiring someone, go ahead and do it, but think of the salary you'll pay your subordinate as an investment on a six-month basis. Keep records as to what this person is doing to increase your business or to free you to generate more clients. Most intelligent stock market investors keep fairly precise figures on how their money is paying off, and you should do the same with the money you're paying your staff.

Part-time help is hard to come by these days, but there are at least two sources of talent to explore. There are a number of bright women who have been married, raised a family, and are now looking for something to do for three or four hours a day. Another group are older people who have retired and want to keep a hand in the business world without devoting all their time to a job. They may want to limit their employment because they don't want to jeopardize their Social Security check by earning too much, or they may just be interested in relaxing in the sun for half the day. Whatever the reason, you have a burgeoning pool of ex-managers whom you couldn't hire for $40,000 on a full-time basis, but who are willing to work for very little, part-time, just to keep their minds active.

When you've made the decision to hire, what sort of personal qualities should you look for in an employee? Once you've found a person who has all the usual qualifications like intelligence, diligence, experience, and dependability, the most important feature in a capable subordinate is good judgment. I place an extremely high value on the person who can make a decision without coming to me to check every detail. Like any human being, I also forget things. I may tell my assistant, Lee Ray, to do something, but when she gets into the job, she may realize, Say, wait a minute. When Mr. Linkletter told me this, I don't think he thought of this other matter. Then she'll call that other matter to my attention, and we may decide not to proceed with the project.

It's that person who can think independently and critically—who can say "Wait a minute" and catch my mistakes—that I look for when I'm hiring or promoting. Walt Disney was another person who prized good judgment in his employees, but he didn't always get it. I'll never forget one amusing incident, when Walt had invited me to be Master of Ceremonies over at ABC-TV for the opening of Disneyland. Halfway through the hour show, he had to cut through a back section of the park to reach a spot where I was waiting for him. But as he moved through this restricted area, he encountered a guard who shouted, "Stop!"

"I've got to get through," Disney said impatiently.

But the guard replied, "My strict orders are that I can't let *anybody* get through here."

"Do you know who I am?" Walt was boiling.

"Yes sir," the guard replied. "You're Walt Disney."

"And you mean to say you're going to stop me?" Walt responded, incredulous.

"Yes sir. I was told to stop everybody."

"Either I go through, or I hit you right in the nose!" Disney growled and charged through. You can imagine that this employee didn't score too highly on his boss's rating of good judgment.

My son Jack, who is president of Linkletter Enterprises, has been president of the Young Presidents Organization, and also now stars on NBC-TV's "America Alive" show, found a number of other factors, in addition to judgment, that are important in hiring a new employee. For one thing, he always tries to avoid hiring people who have the same characteristics and strengths he does. "But it's hard to do," he notes. "Any president who is worth anything puts a great value on the same characteristics that make him good. As a result, I see a lot of companies in the $30 to $40 million class that have a number of top executives with identical personality profiles. If I were a venture capitalist, I would be wary of investing in them because I think these companies are very vulnerable. There's an old saying that expresses this idea as well as I can say it, 'If a guy doesn't think differently from me, he doesn't have anything to offer me.'"

Another type of person whom Jack tries to avoid is the man or woman with psychological quirks that don't fit into his style of management. "If people have the right attitude and sufficient motivation, I'll go a long way in investing time and money in them," he says. "But I won't put them on the psychologist's couch. Take the guy who feels he's superior to the secretaries and clerks in the office. His tone is demanding, and he alienates people. I can't go along with that. I put a lot of time into working on the mix of personalities in our company, and I don't have time for the insecure person who is inclined to abuse the people below him. There are personality traits we develop in childhood that are too hard for a person in my position to change. A businessman should be a businessman and not try to become a psychoanalyst as well."

When you've finally found the person you think will fit into your company, the next challenge that faces you is to motivate him to work for your business as though it were his own. I've found the best way to achieve this kind of motivation is actually to make the person a limited partner with you, in one sense or another. For example, you might offer your employee a percentage of your net earnings, as a sort of profit-sharing arrangement. Or you might actually offer him a percentage of your stock. The man who runs my Australian properties makes a share of the profits we earn, and I think that's my best insurance that those sheep and cattle stations 14,000 miles away are going to do as well as possible.

As a general rule of thumb, I think the percentage you offer a key employee should be in the 10 percent range. If you give him much more, you won't be able to give an adequate amount to any other worker without endangering your complete control of the company. On the other hand, if you give him only 1 percent or 2 percent, there won't be a sufficient amount to make him feel that he's really participating in a significant way with you. Naturally, the final percentage figures depend on the size of the company, the equity capital, etc.

At Linkletter Enterprises, Jack offers what he calls a "cafeteria" approach to employee participation. Employees are entitled to bonuses in good years, but they can select three or four ways to be paid. A young fellow, who has just gotten married and is building a house, may want to take his bonus in cash—say $5000. The executive vice-president, who is more interested in part ownership, may elect to take a percentage of several of the projects we've built. Other people prefer to take their bonuses in the form of extra time off—a long vacation to spend with their families, for example. Finally, Jack will pay an employee's way to take a course at some school if he prefers to further his education.

This approach to worker participation in the business recognizes the importance of partnership as a motivational tool, but differences in interests and ambitions of individual employees are also taken into consideration.

Finally, perhaps the most important kind of participation—even more important than money for many people—is the opportunity to take part in policy meetings and decisions. People need to be recognized as intelligent and important to the operation of the enterprise, and it's also important to demonstrate through your actions that you value their opinions and contributions. An example of how *not* to make a subordinate feel appreciated occurred recently when a president of a major American corporation failed to react at all! His aide had presented an extremely well-researched, lucid report, and got no response from the president.

"I'm surprised that you didn't compliment that young man on the tremendous job he did," the executive vice-president commented.

"Yes, I did," the president replied.

"How?"

"I didn't criticize him."

Personally, I think such an approach is all wrong. Nobody is going to take a lack of criticism to be an implied compliment. People need positive, explicit stroking and reassurances about their performances, as well as monetary bonuses and promotions.

Another important principle in getting the most out of your employees is to help them become as independent as possible, yet with clear and detailed standards of the kind of performance you expect from them. When you delegate a task to a subordinate, you have to learn to take your hands off and let him rise or fall on his own. The best managers delegate responsibility and authority so that the assistant can proceed without worrying that his superiors are always looking over his shoulder. You, at the same time, must remain accountable to your boss or the stockholders for the ultimate result of the employees's job.

I shall never forget a dinner party where I had a lengthy conversation with Lord Hives, chairman of the board of the Rolls-Royce company. He told me that as he approached retirement, his toughest job—the hardest thing he had ever done in his life—was to let his future successor run the company while Hives was away on business trips. He managed to restrain his natural tendency to hop in and correct the younger man's faulty decisions, even when he saw the company might lose some money. He realized that it was essential for his successor to get the feeling of being the pilot in charge of the entire ship so that he would be prepared to take over the whole operation when the time came.

As the employer, your way of assuring that a high level of performance will be maintained is to establish standards which enable the subordinate to look at what he's accomplished and see precisely how he measures up. Jack Linkletter, for example, has broken down each of the jobs at Linkletter Enterprises into certain sets of minimum standards so that when an employee is asked how everything is going, he doesn't have to respond with a "just fine," or some other abstraction. Instead, he can say, "I'm behind on bringing in these new accounts, ahead in this other area," and so on. Establishing precise ways to measure how a task is being executed helps give the subordinate a better feeling about what he's doing, and it also encourages more open, well-defined employee-employer relations.

To give the worker a sense that he's helping to set the standards himself, Jack frequently brings in prospective employees to work for a week or so on a consulting basis. He tells them to analyze the job he's considering them for (though they are not aware this is the job they may move into), and he often brings in another prospect to do the same analysis so that he'll have some basis for comparing performances. Part of the assignment is to write up standards of performance for the position. When the experiment is finished, the company has a valuable job analysis, and except for changes Jack wants to make himself, the employee has actually drawn up his own set of standards.

Another important principle in getting the most out of subordinates and co-workers is always to admit your weaknesses. If you give the impression you know everything there is to know, your employees will be afraid to chime in with their views. Acknowledging your inadequacies makes you more human and encourages others to take more initiative.

I had a partner once who was a highly competent businessman, and we did quite well in our enterprises. But he had the annoying habit, when we got involved in a meeting, of always quickly saying, "Yes, I know," when

I brought up subjects relating to our business. His affirmative responses got on my nerves because I was sure in several cases that he really knew nothing about the subjects that he was claiming to understand.

So I decided to set a trap for him. I said, "That property in the San Fernando Valley which this dairy . . ."

"Oh, yes," he said. "Right out there."

"It's at the cross section of . . ." and I named a precise location.

"Yes, I know."

"That isn't where it is at all!" I said and hesitated for a moment when I saw his face fall. But I knew I had to finish what I had started: "Look, old buddy, you aren't expected to know everything! Let's not kid each other. Both of us can't know it all! I know that I don't. As a matter of fact, it could be costly—this nodding of the head you do all the time. I might go on to something else, assuming you know something you don't, and we'll end up omitting to do something important. Let's both admit our ignorance when we're discussing details of a deal—right?"

As a matter of fact, it's a good idea to carry this principle a step further: Even if you know everything that your subordinates are talking about, it's sometimes a good idea to fail to contribute or actually feign ignorance to give other people a chance to develop their decision-making powers.

Still another way to multiply your outreach is to bring the spouses of your workers in as your allies. Many corporations, for example, increase their sales by offering prizes that would benefit the salesman's wife more than the salesman—mink coats, jewelry, a refrigerator, and so forth. The wife then is more likely to ask the salesman how he's doing on the road and perhaps prod him to greater productivity in weekend selling trips.

Finally, perhaps the most effective way to motivate employees to high levels of performance, especially in creative fields, is to give them public credit for their work. Norman Lear, the producer-writer, uses this approach. In a field where creative workers tend to be ego-driven and marquee-minded, Lear has built an empire by delegating not only many of the original writing and idea-generating chores, but also by giving his people full credit for their creativity. His name remains on the production empire, but his employees have every opportunity to make a name for themselves, as well as to make a lot of money. His approach is quite a contrast to that of Walt Disney, who, with all his strengths, overlooked this deep-seated need of the inventive person to build a separate reputation. Everything that came from his studios was a Disney creation, and as a result, some imaginative people, nursing hurt egos, preferred not to work for him.

These are just a few general guidelines that I've found helpful in building a team that can help you multiply your own talents and effectiveness on the job. These days, it almost always takes more than one person to make a significant impact in any field. The more the daily burdens of the job can be removed from your shoulders, the more time you have to step back and evaluate where you're going and to spend time developing new ideas. The process of reflection is an absolutely essential prerequisite to excellent work, and reflection is impossible without the presence of aides who can provide you with the time to make it possible.

CHAPTER 18

The Art of Selling Yourself

Many people make the mistake of assuming that only professional salesmen need to know the techniques of salesmanship. In fact, *every* successful person is a good salesman in one way or another.

You're constantly trying to convince your business colleagues, your family, or your friends to do something for you—or even just to like you. When you apply for a new job or for a promotion, you certainly have to sell yourself. When a wife tries to talk her prudish husband into going to an R-rated movie, or when a husband tries to sell his wife on the idea that she's too fat for a mink coat —that's really selling! As a matter of fact, one of the most successful salesmen I know actually sold his wife on feeling sorry for the poor girl who lost her earrings in the back seat of the family car!

Of course, not all selling these days is done on a personal, face-to-face basis. Advertising firms push complex marketing plans as well as corporate images on the public through billboards, commercials on radio and television, and through other contemporary communications techniques.

One of the greatest—even if unorthodox—examples

of persuasion I've ever seen, where techniques of both personal and mass media selling came into play, was a Joe Frazier–Muhammad Ali fight I saw in Las Vegas. Ali, with his garrulous mouth, his extravagant and florid statements to the press, his provocative challenges to Frazier, and his predictions about the outcome of the fight, built that box office into millions of dollars. Two other good fighters, who would just have gone out there and slugged it out, could never have accomplished such a feat. Ali, in other words, was a fantastic salesman for my friend, Jack Kent Cook, who put up the $4.5 million for that fight. Ali's loud mouth got the spectators involved. People either got mad, or laughed their insides out, or experienced some other intense emotion. They couldn't wait to get to the arena to see how the contest would come out.

I started to learn the techniques of professional selling when I was about ten years old. We had just moved to Southern California, and I caught the eye of an ice-cream-stand man—primarily because of the dramatic way I could lick an ice cream cone. He offered me ten cents each afternoon, plus all the ice cream I could eat, if I would wander through a nearby park and lick my cones. I used such a seductive curling action with my tongue that passers-by couldn't resist, and the stand's business began to soar. Even to this day, I lick ice cream with the same flourish I used as a kid—despite the fact that my wife has tried, unsuccessfully, for the last thirty years to break me of the habit.

This early success, which launched me on a lifetime of selling, led to the usual newspaper boy routes—an experience I recommend for every youngster because it involves the most challenging of sales jobs, the door-to-door approach. This kind of selling develops such strong character traits as persistence and devotion to responsibility because it's one of the most ego-defeating lines of work in existence. People don't want to be sold anything at their doors, and their first impulse is to shut the door in your face. You have to learn quickly how to make a very fast approach, get their interest immediately, and hold it against overwhelming odds.

Although the life of a newspaper boy was quite independent, I decided to embark on an even more autonomous entrepreneurial project at the very mature age of twelve. We lived in San Diego, and I had been fascinated by some of the things that went on at a place called Lemon Grove, just outside the city. Lemon Grove was the center of lemon-packing plants, where the best lemons were packed and shipped back east. The imperfect lemons, which had spots that made them rot prematurely or scale that caused deterioration, were piled twelve feet high, in rows hundreds of feet long.

These rotting lemons, or "culls," caused a stench that could be smelled for blocks. But, I couldn't help wondering whether some of those lemons—at least, those that still had a shelf life of a few hours—might be put to some good use. Then the idea hit me: Why not sort out as many fairly good lemons as I could find and sell them, door-to-door, at a lower price than that offered by any of the grocery stores?

I got a couple of gunny sacks and began to hitchhike each day from my home to Lemon Grove, which was ten miles away. I'd fill up the sacks and take them back to my backyard, where I dumped them into my mother's washtub. Then I would scrape off the scale, inspect them to find the best ones, and sell them door-to-door. My business became so successful that I had to hire a sales crew of three or four younger boys who would help me with the selling for a 50 percent cut of the price of the lemons. The most important secret of our success was that we kept a very accurate map of where we'd been so we could be sure *never* to go back to the same territory.

These early selling experiences led me to a career in which I've sold in more different ways and to more kinds of people than I can count. I calculated just the other day that during the last forty-five years, I've persuaded a total aggregate audience of more than 50 billion people on radio and television: On the "People Are Funny" show, for example, I not only starred, but personally did commercials every Friday night for nineteen straight years on NBC. These stunt shows were on fifty-two weeks a year, before an average audience of 12 to 14 million people. The numbers were even larger for the "House Party" show: Five days a week, fifty-two weeks a year for twenty-five years, to a daytime audience of 8 to 10 million a day. I've sold live audiences of up to 19,000 on positive-thinking concepts; I've addressed incurable lepers on Pacific islands in an effort to convince them life could be meaningful, even with such a terrible disease; and I've "sweated" my share of "turkeys," or flops, when I'd show up at a giant arena where 10,000 people were supposed to be awaiting my funny audience participation gags, but instead only a handful were present!

And there have been even tougher challenges—such as the time I addressed inmates of an insane asylum, where they divided the audience into separate groups of a hundred or so, with wide spaces between each section. One group would fall down laughing when I walked on stage and said "Hello," while another would begin to scream obscenities. I also spoke at the Squaw Valley Winter Olympics to athletes and trainers from all over the world, where each table had a different language and interpreter. When I'd finished the payoff line of a story, the laughter would burst sporadically, from here, there, and everywhere, because it would take each interpreter a different amount of time to translate what I had said. (The English, of course, laughed last.)

This experience in selling products, concepts, and myself to such a variety of people has impressed me with seven key rules for salesmanship which everyone—professional salesperson or not—should learn to apply.

1. ALWAYS BE ENTHUSIASTIC. If you aren't enthusiastic, the person you're trying to persuade to give you a job or buy your product will fail to see any spark in your personality, and he'll think the less of you for it. If you *force* yourself to act enthusiastic, you'll actually become enthusiastic. I can't tell you how many times I've walked out before a group when I was feeling psychologically low. But when I begin to tell jokes, I leave the stage with an attitude that is 100 percent more positive. Walter Chrysler once said that when salesmen get excited, they get their customers more excited, and the company sells more cars. I know from experience that this principle is true.

2. SHOW EMPATHY FOR THE OTHER PERSON. "Crawl" inside someone else's skin so you can see his point of view. This is a very difficult thing to do because everyone is different and unique. You may see the exact same thing I do but come to an entirely different conclusion about what it means.

One example that illustrates this principle is the story of the four men looking at a sunset. One of them, an artist, says, "What a beautiful painting that would make —such perfect composition and brilliant colors!" A geologist standing next to him, however, observes, "It's interesting how the sun is reflected against that upthrust promontory of land. I wonder what minerals are present there." The third person, a poet, says, "A setting sun reminds me of the warm and beautiful ending of one phase of our lives, and the beginning of another stage at sunrise." Finally, a businessman cocks his head at the colorful horizon and murmurs, "What a view—if we built a hamburger stand here!"

The ability to understand and evoke emotions, to encourage the other person to get *totally* involved in the message you're trying to convey, is necessary. Reason is probably *not* the basic human response to outward conditions and pressures. Human beings originally came out of caves where fear, anxiety, love, and other primitive emotions were the ruling factors in their lives. So, you must go beyond reason and tap these deep reservoirs of emotion if you hope to establish an empathetic relationship with the people you're trying to influence. For example, try to do research on an important business prospect to learn whether he responds best to a hard or soft sell and whether he likes to get right down to business or ease into a business discussion with some casual conversation and jokes. By getting inside the other guy's mind and looking out at the world from his viewpoint, you're much more likely to present yourself to him in a way that will make him respond positively. Remember: The only way to make anyone do something is to make him *want* to do it.

3. RESEARCH WHAT YOU'RE SELLING AND ORGANIZE YOUR PRESENTATION. You can't convince an employer you're

worth promoting if you walk into an interview without knowing the subject matter under discussion. By the same token, it makes little difference how much you know about a product or topic if you can't express yourself clearly and compellingly.

These points were impressed on me most dramatically several years ago when I decided to embark on a cross-country, anti-drug campaign, after my daughter Diane's death. But I soon realized that the fact I had been the victim of a tragedy didn't qualify me as an expert on the subject. I had to learn my product—the nature and terminology of drug abuse among the young. If I got up to talk to a group of high school or college students about drugs and didn't know the differences among "uppers" and "downers" and "speed," or if I tried to tell them they could become addicted to marijuana in the same way they could get addicted to heroin, I would have been laughed off the stage.

I devoted months to studying and listening to the problems of drug use in this country. I shall never forget a visit to a psychiatric ward in a hospital where I experienced the blank stare of a beautiful sorority girl who had been catatonic since she consumed some LSD which had been slipped into her drink by pranksters at a party. I talked with mumbling, nodding heroin addicts in the ghettos of Brooklyn. I comforted agonized parents whose children had died from overdoses of drugs. In other words, I learned in minute detail what drugs in this country were all about. And that extensive research was invaluable as I spoke before young people who had more practical experience with drug use than I did.

But I also found that the wealth of information I had gathered could become confusing and actually make it more difficult to communicate my position unless I took some time before each presentation to get my thoughts organized and to decide on the most important point for each type of audience. Most subjects, especially drugs, are multifaceted, and the mark of an effective communicator is how well he selects key facts for each set of listeners. If pot was a primary problem in one school, then I would slant my talk in that direction instead of spending most of my time on heroin. On the other hand, if cocaine was the "in" drug for another group, I would stress that and downplay other aspects of drug abuse. Parents required an entirely different kind of treatment than adolescents.

Arguing against drug abuse is a gigantic and endless job, and it's not the first thing most people think of when their minds turn to salesmanship. But it's been one of the most challenging and rewarding sales jobs of my life.

4. BE SINCERE. No matter what you're trying to sell or whom you're trying to convince, if you appear to be reciting "canned" lines or trying to put something over on the other guy, you've lost before you even get started. Consumers these days are getting wary. They're skeptical and cynical whenever anyone tries to change their minds, or to get them to buy something new. So if you hope to sell yourself to another person, you have to establish your sincerity immediately and hold that other person's confidence until you reach the point where you ask him to take some action or do something for you.

Generally speaking, sincerity isn't something you can fake—at least, not for any appreciable period of time. If you present a phony front to another person, you may fool him for a little while. But in any long-term relationship, he'll see right through you. There are two fundamental ways to create a genuine kind of sincerity in yourself: First of all, it's necessary to learn your product so well that you're able to discover some aspects of it you can believe in as intensely as you believe in anything. Effective public relations, which is another form of selling, must be based on the same principle. An increasing number of corporations are recognizing this fact by reserving seats on their boards of directors for public relations specialists. Corporate policy is formulated with an eye to what the public wants and what consumer standards are in vogue. In this way, salesmen out in the field, as well as advertisers and public relations firms hired by the company, can say with complete sincerity that their company stands for this or that, or their product was built with such and such a standard in mind. "We know because that's what the board of directors voted at their last meeting."

The second way to engender sincerity is to establish a genuine personal relationship with the individual you're trying to convince. This kind of relationship goes beyond mere manipulation or using the other person to get what you want. Instead, it involves getting to know the other person simply for his or her own sake and also disclosing some personal information about your own background.

One of the most memorable examples of this approach in my own experience occurred when I was representing the Roma Wine Company at the World's Fair in San Francisco in the 1930s. I put on a "World's Fair Party" featuring interviews with interesting personalities to promote the company on radio once a week, and one of my most unusual guests was a circus giant named Jack Earl, who was eight and a half feet tall. He was a charming and bright guy, and I was so impressed by him, I took him out to dinner afterwards. He told me he was quitting the circus because it was too demeaning, but he was worried about what sort of a normal job a guy his size could get.

"Have you ever thought of selling?" I asked.

"What could I sell?" he replied.

"You're talking to the man who represents the world's biggest winery," I said, as an idea began to form in my mind. "I'm wondering why the biggest company shouldn't have the biggest salesman? We could have some oversized calling cards made up, and you could walk into the stores where we sell and be the come-on for a really effective sales message."

He liked the idea and soon was walking into those stores and giving as good a pitch as any salesman I've heard, but he had one extra thing in his favor. His prospective customers were always eager to hear Jack's life story—about his circus days and the problems such a big man faces in a small-scale world. In other words, his height gave him a tremendous advantage in establishing genuine personal relationships and in communicating the sincerity that arises most naturally from such relationships.

5. GOOD SALESMEN ARE GOOD INTERVIEWERS. I've discovered that when you're trying to persuade someone to do something for you or buy a product you're pushing, one of the best approaches is to interview *him*. Ask a series of questions to elicit opinions and facts from him. This tactic serves at least four major purposes: One of the most flattering things you can do for a person is to ask his opinion about something, because you're implicitly saying, "I think you're a knowledgeable person with some important things to say." While he's bragging or

talking about himself, you're getting a good impression of what he wants, and that should help you find your key selling point with him. If he's doing the talking and you're not saying much, that also helps you avoid saying things that may alienate him and lead to a disagreement. Finally, if you're only asking questions, you're more likely to keep from talking too much and becoming a bore.

I first became fascinated by the craft of interviewing because I wanted to be a radio star, but I had no outstanding, visible talent like dancing or singing to catapult me to fame and fortune. My problem, when I first started out in show business, was that I was a radio announcer, and in those days, being an announcer was like being the man at the front desk at the MGM Grand Hotel; I had the biggest desk in the building, but I wasn't very important. I was just a front man to introduce all the talented people who came on to perform.

But then I heard a brand-new show called "Vox Pop," over CBS. It was a voice-of-the-people program where an interviewer would take a microphone into the street and interview people on different subjects. That program struck a responsive note in me because I immediately thought, That's something I've been doing all my life without realizing it could be considered entertainment. So I started inserting street interviews in my radio programs, and my "learning curve" in the art of selling myself to interview subjects began almost at once. In fact, the first guy I approached with a question turned out to be a drunk who roared, "What the hell do you care?" Since then, I've probably interviewed more people than anyone else in the broadcasting industry. Sometimes the conversations broke out into fist fights, and other interviews required me to overcome the ravings of insane people.

I've become more convinced every year in my later business life that an interviewing background is an invaluable addition to anyone's repertoire of selling skills.

6. EMPLOY DEMONSTRATIONS WHENEVER POSSIBLE. Some of the most effective selling occurs after you've gotten as many of the other person's senses involved as possible. You'll communicate more memorably and convincingly if your subject can see, hear, taste, touch, or smell what you're trying to get across.

For example, one young engaged couple walked into a china shop to look at some Wedgwood bone china for their first kitchen. The young man was bored because he didn't know or care anything about china, but the salesman knew he would have a better chance of making the sale if he could get the fellow involved. So he said, "Look at this cup. Isn't it delicate and fragile? Now watch. . . ." He then put the cup upside down on the floor and stood on it without breaking it.

The salesman knew that his weight would be evenly distributed over the cup in a way that would easily support him. The young man's response was just what the salesman had expected: "Hey, how about that! That's *some* cup!"

A similar example of demonstration selling is the insulation retailer who waits until the first snow and then drives around town until he sees a bare roof. He calls the owner of the house outside and says, "Look at your roof!"

"What about it?" the owner replies.

"Look at the other houses around here—there's snow on top of them, but you don't have any. You're heating your roof and melting the snow on top. That means something's wrong with your insulation. I'll bet the other people around here are paying lower heating bills than you are, too. Now let me tell you something about the insulation services I can offer you. . . ."

The use of demonstrations can be effective in many other situations as well. When you're applying for a job, for example, it's always a good idea to have a copy of your resume (even if you've already sent one in advance) or perhaps something you've produced on another job, such as a published article or brochure. Put these items in the hands of your prospective employer, so that he'll have something concrete to hold and examine as you proceed with your job interview. Or if you're making a report to a group of your superiors, have copies of graphs, a slide show, or some other demonstration. This approach will both encourage them to get personally involved in your report and also give the impression that you've put a good deal of time and effort into the presentation.

My first exposure to demonstration selling—and this was demonstration with a strong touch of the empathy approach—occurred when I was only seven years old. My father, who adopted me as he wandered through Canada in 1912, was both a shoemaker and an evangelist. (I used to say he saved one kind of soul on Sundays and an entirely different set of soles during the week.) He was an old-style preacher who believed in selling salvation with as effective an emotional pitch as he could muster. My job in his services, as a small, skinny, under-fed youngster, was to take up the collection. This role was particularly important because, like the families of many traveling ministers, we had to live on those Sunday offerings from week to week.

When the time for the collection arrived, he would introduce me by saying something like this: "As you good people know, we traveling evangelists have to live on the love offerings that fine congregations like yours give us. One of my own children, who will be eating the very food that your generous gifts buy, will be moving among you now, and I would encourage you to respond as God moves you. . . ."

Then, wearing old clothes (all I had), I would walk up and down the aisles with a big offering plate, and I'd turn my little hollow-cheeked face up to them and stare them in the eye until they dropped something into the plate. Demonstration selling, in other words, actually put food on our table when I was just a youngster, and it's been an integral part of my selling techniques ever since.

7. BE COURAGEOUS IN CLOSING YOUR SALE. Many good salesmen often fail at the conclusion of their sales presentations because they're afraid to ask for the order. Whether you're an evangelist, a shoe salesman, or an upwardly mobile corporation employee looking for a promotion, you have to ask people directly for what you want, or it's likely you'll never receive it. Most people like to avoid making decisions, especially if the decision is important and money is involved. So if you want to sell yourself, an idea, or some product to another individual, it is usually up to you to make the final move—to push the other person toward a decision. You might say, "I'm wondering if I could have an increase in my salary," or "I'd very much like to have this job," or "I recommend the company do this or that." If your potential buyer can't or won't make a final decision on the spot, be aggressive in getting in touch with him a week later or at some other predetermined time and apply tactful pressure to prod him toward a final decision.

It often requires good organization and a bright personality to get your ideas across in a sales presentation. But getting the person's name on a sheet of paper and getting his check in your hand require character and courage. These qualities are what you need to round out your ability to sell yourself effectively.

These seven rules should be of particular help to you when you're trying to sell yourself and your ideas in the broadest sense of the word "sell." But if you work in sales or think you might like to, here are some additional, more specialized principles which should help you enhance the marketability of your product:

USE CATCHY, MEMORABLE PHRASES. Advertising and direct mail specialists always try to catch the essence of their product in a word, phrase, or short sentence that will echo in the potential customer's mind and surface in the form of a concrete sale.

When I was representing the Roma Wine Company at the San Francisco World's Fair, I was casting around for just such a slogan, and it finally appeared from an unusual source. My father, who had been inveighing for years as a minister against any kind of booze, was a little disconcerted when I told him I'd be representing a wine company. But he finally reconciled himself to the idea by relying on St. Paul's advice to Timothy to "use a little wine for the sake of your stomach," and Jesus' miracle of turning the water into wine at the Cana wedding. But he cautioned me to try to sell my alcoholic products temperately.

So I went back to the office, and intent on devising an advertising concept that would mollify dear old Dad, I came up with a highly successful slogan: "Don't drink it—sip it!" An entire advertising campaign was built around these words, and as a result, Roma's sales chart took a leap upward. My father was happy, too, because he could tell his friends, "My son says, 'Don't drink it!'"

INCLUDE A PREMIUM. My next sponsor, equally distasteful to my father, was the Wings cigarette company. I was approached by a representative of this company about thirty years ago, well before any of the current cancer research, and was asked to sell for them on radio. But I replied, "I won't go on the air and say I smoke, because I don't. I don't believe in it. I don't really think they're good for you."

The elderly cigarette representative replied, with a twinkle in his eye, "Possibly—even probably. But people are going to smoke cigarettes anyway, and we have this wonderful way of selling them—through premiums. You don't have to say you smoke. Just tell them when they buy a pack, they get coupons which can be exchanged for gifts."

Fascinated by this sales technique, I accepted the offer and was constantly amazed at how responsive the public was to buying items that had a premium, or free gift, attached. This principle continues to be as valid today as it was when I first learned the approach. Direct mail experts and other salespeople are consistently finding, through scientifically conducted tests, that their products sell better with even the most inexpensive premium than they do without one.

LOOK FOR AN UNTAPPED MARKET. All too often, salesmen beat their heads against the wall, trying to sell their products to people who are already oversold. But with a little thought and research, you may find a vast, untapped reservoir of customers who can be your ticket to immediate success in the sales field. It's often just a matter of taking a step back, carefully examining your potential market, and then having the courage to step out and risk failure with untried consumers.

One experience I had involved some selling I was asked to do for the Pillsbury cake mix people. The concept of a cake mix that you could buy in a box, combine with some milk, and cook for a while to get a tasty cake was foreign to the American way of thinking before the Pillsbury company entered the field. Americans seemed to have almost a religious attitude toward cakes: Every good mother had her own secret formula, and the idea of undercutting her personal sense of identity as a homemaker seemed almost sacrilegious to some people. Pillsbury called in psychologists to study the problem, and some felt we were toying with emotional dynamite with our new mix. In fact, a few argued that a basic factor in the mystique of cake baking was the expression of subliminal sex urges. We even had members of the board of directors and the company president, himself, spending time in the Pillsbury consumer kitchen, baking cakes to see if they were getting any kind of libido stimulation.

"The amazing thing," one executive confided to me with a wink, "is that I *did* feel something! So now if you drop by my house on a weekend, you may just see me sitting there, baking away. . . ."

Despite certain reservations about taking the details of cake making away from the American housewife, we decided to proceed with the cake mix selling program. So I went on the air with my pitch, "Yes, you really can make a cake out of this little box. . . ." And we never had one hint of a problem. Instead of threatening the domain of the traditional cake baker, we found we were catching an entirely different consumer group—those who had never before had any inclination to make their own cakes. The result was a resounding success in a previously untapped market, simply because Pillsbury had executives who possessed the courage to disregard the negative voices and take a risk on an unknown product.

TESTIMONIALS ALWAYS REINFORCE YOUR SALES PITCH. People generally like to buy in a crowd. If they know someone else has purchased a particular product and been satisfied, they're much more likely to put down some money themselves. Hence, the value of a testimonial or statement by a prior satisfied customer.

If you walk into someone else's office, send out a direct mail piece, or try to get your message across on television or radio, your approach will probably be effective in direct proportion to the strength of the testimonials you use. Some products sell best when an unknown but obviously genuine person talks about what a great job the product has done for him. Other items move more quickly behind a celebrity testimonial, such as the type the Wheaties people used with decathlon champion Bruce Jenner. As every television viewer knows, he described how often he began his days as a kid with a Wheaties breakfast—and look at him now!

Finally, when you walk into a prospective buyer's office, you can strengthen your position by using a testimonial from someone he knows personally, "I just sold this same computer system to Mr. Jones, whom I think you know, of the XYZ company, and he's quite happy. . . ."

The testimonial is especially effective if you're trying to push a new, revolutionary product that is so unusual you're afraid no one will want to be the first to try it.

The idea is to get someone else to try it and speak favorably about it, so that your first regular customers don't have to be the first. I faced this situation in pushing the Toni home permanent, which advised women, for the first time in history, to open a bottle of chemicals and pour them on their hair. Our lawyers were beside themselves as they visualized lawsuits by people who had burned or frizzed their hair beyond repair. When I went on the air, I used the testimonial approach to selling by going out with my microphone and interviewing people on street corners who had used the product and whose hair, far from dropping out, looked beautiful. The result was a set of personal endorsements that sold the home permanents beyond the Toni company's wildest dreams and drastically changed the beauty habits of American women. Having used testimonials many times since then, I've always found them to improve the image of the products I'm trying to push—and that's my own personal testimonial for the testimonial.

STRESS WHAT LOOKS GOOD MORE THAN WHAT'S GOOD FOR YOU. Unfortunately, the public seems to respond more readily to things which enhance the outward appearance, often without any regard for the basic health, intellectual, or spiritual benefits of the product. Even if you have an item that will improve the inner man, you often have to stress the outward, more superficial aspects of what it does to get the consumer to put his money on the line.

I discovered this truth while serving on the board of directors for the Royal Crown Cola company. At the time I joined the board, the company desperately needed a new image to help it compete more effectively with Coca-Cola and Pepsi. I visited every bottling plant in the country and talked regularly to groups of several dozen to a hundred sleepy driver-salesmen at 6:30 in the mornings, trying to convince them that R.C. was a big and important company they should be proud to work for. Then, I'd stay over for luncheon meetings with the plant managers and town officials and their spouses and wax eloquent on the fun of selling soda pop.

Something, however, was missing from all the enthusiasm I was trying to generate. No matter how inspirational I tried to be, there was nothing that distinctive we had to offer. It seemed that whatever claims we could make, the two other larger companies would say the same things but more often and on bigger networks. Then one day, as I was visiting the Research and Development department at R.C., I came across a drink that was still being developed. It had been tentatively called "Diet Rite," it tasted great, and it was supposed to have only two calories.

"This is what we need!" I exclaimed. "This is a Unique Selling Proposition. Let's get it on the market!"

The R and D people responded that they still needed to work on it awhile, but I insisted it be put on the market immediately—except I believed that we should change the name. "Diet Rite is a lousy name," I said. "The idea of dieting means you have to discipline yourself, and nobody wants to do that. The most important thing is that there's no sugar in it, and that should be good in preventing cavities in your teeth. Most of these drinks are drunk by kids, not adults, so it's the kid market we've got to hit."

As it turned out, I was wrong on both counts. We did get an endorsement from the American Dental Association, but it was mostly adults who bought it because of the diet concept. The name "Diet Rite" went right to the heart of the most effective sales approach. People showed they were most interested in their own appearance, their own figures. They didn't care if the word "diet" carried connotations of discipline, and they also apparently didn't care too much about what happened to their kids' teeth. So even though there may have been a healthful side effect, the important thing to these consumers was appearance—specifically the effect the product would have on the way their own bodies looked.

STRESS A PRACTICAL AND DIRECT SALES PITCH. Vagueness and indirection never sold anybody anything. Children learn immediately that if they're going to sell cups of lemonade to passers-by in front of their house, they have to get to the point: It's necessary, at least, to put up a sign such as "Lemonade for sale, 15¢ a glass." Or better yet, they should approach the stranger directly with a sales pitch. But I doubt that any lemonade has ever been sold by a child who just sits on his front lawn with a pitcher, without some direct approach to encourage pedestrians or drivers to turn over their money.

Unfortunately, many grownups have never learned this lesson either. I used to work for General Electric on the "House Party" show, but they were never quite comfortable with my approach. In the first place, they didn't like the way I rummaged through ladies' purses on the air, nor were they particularly enamored with the fact that I'd ask kids, "What do your mother and daddy do for fun?" The answer I'd get would often be something like, "How do I know—they always lock the door!"

"That's just not our image, Art," they told me. They

wanted something a little more refined and cultured. But despite their dissatisfaction, they kept my show on the air for five years for one simple reason: I sold their merchandise. Whatever we advertised on our program—the toasters, electric blankets and other items that I picked up and showed to consumers who were watching the TV set—had a way of moving on the shelves of the nation's stores.

But G.E. finally decided that what they gained with my direct, pocketbook approach didn't offset the informal image I gave them, so they dropped my show and brought on Fred Waring and the Pennsylvanians. That show certainly projected more of an aura of class and style, but they were on for only thirteen weeks! Cancelled because they weren't getting through to the masses. They weren't selling the products. In the last analysis, in other words, the success of your approach depends on how well you sell to the consumer's practical needs, not to his intellectual sensitivities. If you want to strive for artistic excellence or construct some abstract theory that has a certain logical symmetry and beauty but no particular practical application, that's fine—even admirable. But don't confuse such pursuits with good salesmanship or expect the general public to come knocking at your door with an overwhelming demand for your creation. The only way you'll have any chance to sell your theory or artwork or literary masterpiece is to apply the rules and techniques of salesmanship discussed in this chapter.

No matter how well you master this art of selling yourself, however, you'll probably never achieve the full success that can be yours unless you become an expert at organizing your time. You may have a winning personality and the intelligence and sensitivity to perceive just which approach should be applied in each situation, but if you're unable to work efficiently and get things done on time, your success will be dramatically limited. Because I place such a tremendous importance on personal organization, I'd like to spend the next few chapters on practical tips for time control.

PART FIVE

Time Control:
Your Basic Tool of Achievement

CHAPTER 19

A Primer on Organizing Your Time

Pages and pages have been written about time management—in large part, I suppose, because this issue is one that nags at the conscience of most of us at one point or another. We're programmed to believe that we should make the most of every minute, but because we're fallible humans, we always waste more time than is good for us. To remedy this defect in our personalities and also, I suspect, to do penance out of a sense of guilt, we buy time books or go to efficiency seminars.

Some of this time management advice is quite good, but I'm skeptical about the ability of anyone to incorporate the comprehensively efficient style of life that many time consultants advocate. Most of us are capable of taking only small steps to correct our wasteful tendencies, so I usually advise a simple set of four fundamentals to help people get better organized. Here they are:

1. KEEP LISTS OF YOUR RESPONSIBILITIES IN A DAILY APPOINTMENT DIARY. At the risk of appearing boastful, I believe I'm one of the best organized people you'll ever meet. And the reason for this organization is not that I have such a sophisticated philosophy of time management, but that I write everything down. I don't trust my

memory with respect to appointments and other obligations, and I also don't want to be bothered by trying to remember where I'm supposed to be or what I should be doing every minute of the day. I keep a master calendar that sometimes runs a year in advance, and all my dates are recorded there so that on a moment's notice, I can accept or turn down new proposals. It's a good idea for your secretary to keep a duplicate diary so that she can answer for you if you're out of town, or you can keep a master diary in the office and carry a duplicate pocket diary with you when you're on trips.

Every Sunday night, I sit down with my appointment diary and go over the activities that will be coming up during the next week. In a typical week, I have something to do in each of seventeen activities including both business and social duties. Often, I find I have to transfer items from the previous week, which are unfinished for one reason or another, to the upcoming week's schedule. Even though some things may not be completed exactly when I had planned, I know they'll eventually get done because they're right there, in black and white, on my weekly schedule where I can't miss them.

But here's one word of caution to keep in mind as you embark on your list-making: Be careful not to overestimate how much you can do in a given day, or you may get discouraged or impose undue anxiety on yourself as you try to meet an unrealistic volume of obligations. If you expect a phone conversation will take twenty minutes, allow thirty to give yourself some leeway. Or if you have one appointment set up on one side of town for 9 A.M. and another on the other side of town for 10:30, be sure you're making a reasonable estimate of how long it will take to cover the distance between the locations.

These may seem like ridiculously self-evident points, but I find that too often, ambitious business people try to squeeze too many meetings into one day, and as a result, they are always anxious, harried, and frequently late.

2. SCHEDULE RELATED TASKS INTO BLOCKS OF TIME, RATHER THAN SPREADING THEM OUT THROUGHOUT THE DAY. Many kinds of work, such as correspondence and telephone conversations, are best lumped together during a predetermined hour or two in the morning or afternoon. By doing them together, you'll find they don't interrupt your other tasks. Also, you can gain a momentum in working on the related tasks, and that should help you handle them more efficiently than if you try to tackle them in fragmented fashion.

I've found this approach to be particularly helpful during my "transition time," when I'm traveling on an airplane or waiting in an airport. You have a half hour, an hour, or more each day, either during commuting or at some other transition stage between meetings, when you usually do nothing. So why not try to fill in that block of dead time with some constructive activity, like dictating correspondence into a small tape recorder or writing personal notes to friends? I travel about 200,000 miles a year, and I consider the hours I spend on airplanes golden because there's no one to pester me as I catch up on personal correspondence or do creative thinking. With family and business obligations, there's very little chance other than on an airplane to mull over such things as a letter of condolence to a woman whose husband has just died, or a congratulatory note to a friend who has just had a promotion.

3. SCHEDULE FUN AND RECREATION INTO YOUR MONTH. I've found it's absolutely necessary for busy people to

include in their appointment books blocks of time which they plan to spend with their families or with friends in various types of recreation or sports. If you don't plug these things into your program and consider them to be just as important as your business engagements, you'll shortchange yourself in these areas, and your overall state of well-being is bound to suffer.

I love to ski, and I regard vacations on the slopes with my family to be essential to my emotional and physical health. When I had one of these recreation periods scheduled a year or so ago, a company called me up to offer a high-priced speaking assignment in Guam. It would have meant $10,000 plus expenses to me. I couldn't possibly tell these people that I couldn't go because I was going skiing; that would have seemed unbelievable. So I merely said: "I have a business date I can't break. My schedule is completely booked."

I mentioned this incident to a friend a short time later, and he said, "Gosh, that ski trip was worth $10,000 to you?" And I could say with complete honesty, Yes! because I know how important such outings are for my own relaxation and for my relationships with my family.

On a recent trip to New York City, I ran into a cab driver whose view of work and recreation priorities was diametrically opposed to mine. He picked me up at the airport just before midnight, and I asked, "How do you like this late-night cab driving? Do you do it by choice?"

"No," he replied. "I *have* to do it. I have another job during the day and then I work doing this at night. It's a long day, but by gosh, my two kids are going to have a lot of things I never had."

"When do you see them?" I asked.

"Not very often. I work till 5 P.M., change my clothes, and then go right out again. They're asleep when I get home, and they're not even up in the morning when I leave for work."

I didn't comment out loud, but I thought, Here's this poor, sad soul, breaking his neck to give his kids bicycles, tape decks, and other material things when what they really need is *him*. Too often, unless you make a conscious effort to schedule recreation and family time into your life, money-making fills the vacuum. Then you find yourself on a treadmill, rushing through life, getting more and more involved in career responsibilities. Anyone who expects to be successful must devote ample time to renewing his strength. Relaxation, fun, and the ability to pace yourself are key ingredients in sustaining high achievement levels over a long lifetime.

4. EXPECT TO BE PLAGUED BY THINGS BEYOND YOUR CONTROL. Sometimes when I'm sitting in an airport, I notice people worrying themselves into such a state that they get almost physically sick because their plane isn't going to take off on time. I used to get upset by such things, but I learned a number of years ago that there's no point in fussing about something you can't control.

I now have an action plan that I put into effect with late airplanes. I immediately check with other airlines to see if I can switch to another flight. If I can't, I just relax and look upon the unavoidable delay as an unexpected gift of time which I can use to plan my business projects or work on correspondence. Things never move along just as you plan them, because the world is imperfect and unpredictable. The sooner you learn to be resilient and creative when a surprise interruption or delay hits you, the more productive you'll become and the less subject to time-wasting, energy-draining anxiety attacks.

The problem in implementing time tips can often be traced to personal problems which are by no means insuperable but which still must be recognized and dealt with directly if you hope to get control of your time. There seem to be three basic personality types who run into problems with time management—people I refer to as "ants," "sloths," and "swine." Everyone, including myself, has demonstrated one or more of these character traits at some time, so if I seem to be pointing an accusing finger at you, you're right, I am! Take the following test to see which designation best fits your personality.

THE ANT. The ant usually gets high marks in the Bible as an example of diligence to follow. But antlike tendencies, even in the best of us, can run wild if we're not careful. You're probably an ant if you:
- tend to take on too many responsibilities and spread yourself too thin
- have to work longer hours than your co-workers
- can't make ends meet at home unless you work long hours or hold down a second job
- usually can't say no when someone asks you to help him with a job or serve on some committee
- believe few people can do a job as well as you can
- are not happy unless you're working
- don't have any hobbies to speak of
- think it's more pleasant to be at the office than at home with your family
- fear people won't respect you unless you're diligent at work

— feel the key to success is the number of hours you put in at a task

THE SLOTH. At the other end of the spectrum is the person who is the antithesis of diligence and efficiency. No matter how pure his motives, he just can't seem to get down to work and do a decent job with what's assigned to him. You're a sloth if you:

— tend to postpone unpleasant, difficult tasks
— have trouble getting started in the morning
— have never had a job that you really enjoyed
— find your mind wanders a great deal while you're at work
— always feel tired
— usually take more than an hour for lunch
— are almost always fifteen minutes or more late to work
— talk to people in person or on the phone while at work whenever you get a chance
— always take all your sick days, whether you're really ill or not
— are never one minute late in leaving work

THE SWINE. I suppose pigs have something to commend them, but when I think of a pig, images of messiness and disorganization come to mind. Unfortunately, many people display some of these same features in their daily working lives. You're playing the swine if you:

— work fairly hard, but some important tasks always seem to remain unfinished
— often feel as though you're spinning your wheels at work

— have a desk that tends to stay messy, and/or have trouble finding important papers in your files
— get frustrated because you always seem to be weeks behind in your correspondence
— seem incapable of getting the best work out of your secretaries
— never seem to have time to clean out your car, and your clothes closets look like the aftermath of a cyclone
— your family vacations are frequently unsatisfying because you don't plan ahead properly
— have trouble throwing away old magazines, clippings, and paperback books
— never can seem to meet deadlines you set for yourself
— are almost always late to business appointments and other engagements

If you find you fit into two or even three of the categories, don't be too surprised. Some people are ants, sloths, and swine all at once. That just means you have to concentrate more seriously than most others on getting control of your time.

In addition to the four fundamentals mentioned earlier in this chapter, there are also a number of other principles and techniques that apply to specific time management problems. I'd like to explore these with you in the next four chapters to give you some tools for overcoming any time management problems you've detected in yourself.

CHAPTER 20

Why You Should Get Mean
in the Morning

The most effective method I've discovered to accomplish a great deal during any given day is to tackle the hardest tasks first—or "get mean in the morning," as I sometimes put it. Most of us prefer to ease into the day, piddling around with minor, low-priority work until we can open our eyes wide enough to wrestle with important issues. But by that time, it's usually noon, and we may find we haven't really accomplished anything during the morning.

In other words, we organize our business days much as we buy food at a cafeteria: Often, the desserts are at the front of the line to tempt us, and the meat and vegetables —the really important food—are at the other end. In fact, we may pile so many sweets up on the tray that there's no room for the vegetables at all.

Your workday presents a similar problem. If you take on the less challenging jobs in the morning, there may be no time left at the end of the day to do what's really important. Therefore, sit down at the end of each day and decide what is the most unpleasant or difficult responsibility confronting you the next day. Then, grit your teeth and plunge into that assignment, and I guarantee that you'll emerge with a tremendous feeling of accomplishment that will give you sufficient momentum to whiz through your other tasks.

I sometimes find I have to make a call to a business colleague to tell him I've decided not to go ahead with a project, and I'm tempted to put off the call because I know he'll be disappointed. But I've disciplined myself to sit down at the phone the first thing in the morning, ring him up, and get rid of the bad news before I do anything else. Otherwise, the fact that I have to call him will hang over my head for the rest of the day, nag at the back of my mind, and prevent me from throwing my full energies and concentration into other work.

The basic principle underlying this idea is that it's important to arrange your day in order of *descending* priorities. By establishing your priorities ahead of time, you reduce the possibility that you'll arrange your schedule according to the pressures you feel. More often than not, it's the least important things that get in your way and demand your attention. If you've failed to evaluate those jobs and assign them a lower priority, it's likely that the pressures they exert on you will succeed in diverting you from more significant tasks. For example, if you happen to be a telephone addict who has to answer every call, no matter what sort of conference or other job you're involved with, interruptions are going to devastate your attempts to be efficient. On the other hand, if you tell your secretary to hold all your calls, regardless of who it is, and your wife unsuccessfully tries to get through to tell you your son has mangled his hand or fallen down the cellar steps, your family may have good reason to question the priorities you've established for your life. Values and priorities should be subjected to constant scrutiny and reevaluation, and first things should literally be put first to insure that they get finished.

An example of one person who reacted to the pressures of her immediate needs and lost sight of basic human values involved a young girl who married a wealthy old man. She apparently was quite fond of him in the beginning, but then she started focusing on the external demands of maintaining a home. She said, "The garden looks shabby," and he replied, "Okay, we'll spend some money to take care of it."

They brought in a gardening crew, and the grounds soon looked gorgeous. But then the young wife noticed that cutting away the plants and hedges disclosed that the house looked shabby and really needed a paint job. So they called in the painters. Now, the outside of the place was great, but she told her husband, "You know, when you walk inside, you're struck by the shabbiness of the decoration."

"Okay, we'll get a decorator," he sighed.

Finally, when the entire estate—inside and out—sparkled, she decided that her husband looked too shabby, so she got rid of him.

Now, this story may make you smile a little, but the underlying point is even more important than any humor. It's essential that the important things in your life get attention immediately, or you may find you've ignored them so long that it's too late to do anything about them. Your highest priorities should always get the most attention, but if you've never decided what your priorities should be, it's likely you'll never complete them. Instead, you'll probably waste your time on relatively insignificant tasks, and your life will become a pattern of random reactions to pressure, rather than a well-planned road to success.

But even if you can decide on what your highest-priority project should be, and you feel highly motivated to get started on it the first thing in the morning, at least three very difficult obstacles may still get in your way: the job that never gets done, the "painful place" syndrome, and the meandering mind. Here are some suggestions about how to overcome them.

1. THE JOB THAT NEVER GETS DONE. Although it's important to start on your toughest task at the outset each day, some item on your schedule will inevitably keep getting shoved back until you realize, days or weeks later, that you've never touched the job in question.

Much of the pressure and anxiety felt at work comes from these uncompleted tasks. Some psychologists call this "reactive anxiety" because it results from a concrete situation to which you are reacting. If you take care of that situation—in this case, do the job that you've been putting off—the anxiety usually disappears.

The most effective technique to insure that some tasks don't get put off forever involves what is sometimes called the "rotating responsibilities rule." This rule says that you can increase your productivity and maintain a more balanced schedule by putting a new item of business at the top of your schedule each day. In other words, you may put your correspondence first today, your major marketing problem second, and a report for your boss third. But you probably won't finish that report to your boss, so tomorrow, you rotate the order of work: Do the boss's report first, and so on. The result is that you won't work on all the tasks you've planned on any given day, but by rotating jobs, you won't neglect something entirely. Over a period of a week or two, you'll find you're completing everything.

2. THE PAINFUL PLACE SYNDROME. Many people are slow to begin tasks in the morning because they like to avoid office locations that are connected with hard work. These are painful places, such as a desk or a particular office, which you associate with concentration, tough decision-making, and anxiety. Your goal should be to transform these painful places into pleasure places so that it will be easier to go directly there when you first arrive at work.

I know one writer, for example, who had a problem faced by many self-employed people: He couldn't make himself sit down at his typewriter early in the morning. He would make some coffee and plop down on the sofa with the newspaper. Then, after finishing his reading, he'd walk out to check the mailbox to see if the postman had arrived. If his mail had come, he'd bring it back to his living room and spend some time dawdling over it with a second cup of coffee. And if a magazine had come with the mail, that would be still another excuse to postpone the painful experience of sitting down and pounding away at those typewriter keys. It was so much easier to let his mind remain passive, to relax on a soft couch and do some pleasure reading, rather than make that extra effort to become creative and fill up those blank pages of paper on his desk with his priceless prose.

My friend genuinely wanted to "get mean in the morning" and have the satisfaction of knowing that he had put in two or three good hours of work before lunch. But with his bad work habits, he would do well to complete even one hour. Then a behavioral psychologist visited him one weekend, and out of desperation and a sense of guilt that he was wasting too much of his time, the writer poured out his frustrations.

"There are gimmicks you can use to overcome any problem like this," the psychologist said. "So why don't we take a few minutes and figure out the best way to get you seated in front of your typewriter in the morning."

The psychologist suggested that the writer take his coffee cup and newspaper and go directly to his type-writer, rather than stop at the sofa. How much more pleasant for the writer to sit at his desk and sip and read, rather than sit on the sofa with nothing to do. But the subtle difference between the typewriter chair and the sofa was that he associated his office, desk, and typewriter with work, rather than with relaxation, as was the case with the sofa. So his coffee drinking and reading tended to go much faster as he sat in his workroom. In fact, he sometimes skipped the newspaper altogether and got right down to work. The subtle pressure exerted by the surrounding work environment encouraged him to begin work more quickly.

The distractions you face in the morning may be different from what this writer encountered. But a little analysis of the obstacles that keep you from getting off to a fast start is an excellent first step in coming up with some techniques to eliminate those painful places in your life.

3. THE MEANDERING MIND. Even if you plant yourself at your desk, it may be hard to do heavy thinking early in the morning because you may still be in the process of waking up. Or if you're already wide awake, it's diffi-cult sometimes to focus your thoughts on the task at hand because your imagination may lead you to fanta-

size about some compelling topic that is completely irrelevant to your work.

It's important to build momentum as quickly as possible during the first few minutes at your desk because the pace you set at the beginning of the day will often determine the pace at which you work later. To refocus your meandering mind and get off the starting block quickly, here are several techniques that you may find helpful:

When you feel your mind beginning to wander, immediately *overschedule your day.* In other words, take out a pad of paper and block out your day in periods of no more than an hour each. Assign a task, no matter how insignificant, to each of these periods. For example, you might write, 9 A.M.—begin introduction on report for Mr. Jones. 9:30—finish introduction, begin section in report on computer applications to the problem. . . . By breaking the task down into stages and setting a series of short-term deadlines to complete each stage, you'll be more likely to focus on making continual progress toward your ultimate goals at work. And you'll find your mind will be less inclined to wander than if you merely set aside an amorphous block of time of several hours to do the job.

Play mental games to maintain your concentration. For example, if you have to draft several business contracts, imagine you're in a newspaper office with a definite, unalterable deadline for the first contract. Then try to beat that deadline so that you can get a head start on the next responsibility.

Learn to fight early morning fatigue. If you're often tired in the morning, it's almost impossible to begin your day at peak efficiency, so your first concern should be to improve the way you feel. Sometimes the problem is simple: Perhaps you're just not getting enough sleep! Each of us falls into the habit, at one time or another, of watching TV or reading into the wee hours and then expecting we can get up after five or six hours of sleep and go right to work without any impairment of efficiency. In fact, most people need more sleep than this. I know one young woman who frequently felt horrible at work in the morning, and it took three or four cups of coffee and perhaps an hour of staring blankly at the wall before she could get her creaky mental processes sufficiently warmed up to think a coherent thought. At first, she thought she was suffering from some chemical imbalance. Then she discovered she's one of those people who need about nine hours of sleep each night, and getting to bed earlier has made a tremendous difference in her morning work.

I've also heard some people say: "Well, I can't get started in the morning because I'm not a 'morning person.' I'm an 'evening person,' and I guess I'll just have to live with the fact that I'm not going to be efficient when I first sit down at my desk."

There may be some truth to this complaint. I can accept the fact that some people may be constitutionally more capable of doing good work in the morning, or afternoon, or evening, but I don't believe it's impossible to change or reset whatever biological clocks make better workers at a certain time of the day. One friend of mine, who always used to say he was a night person, could do great thinking and working from about 9 P.M. to 2 A.M., but he just didn't feel he was good for anything at all before noon. I thought to myself, How sad! This fellow has to go through his entire life as a kind of occupational cripple! Unfortunately, the way the American capitalist system is set up, most people have to finish half their workday by lunchtime. But then I heard that my friend had discovered distance running, and suddenly he found he had turned into a morning person.

"I would never have believed this was possible!" he told me. "I get up almost every morning and run four or five miles before breakfast, and I'm so wide-awake and energetic by the time I sit down to work that I now get my best work done before noon."

I don't regard the morning–night person argument as an immutable law of nature, and here's one final note on the benefits of physical activity in overcoming fatigue in the morning or any other time of the day, for that matter. Some people often feel their commitment to their jobs should be measured by the amount of time they keep their bottoms on a chair in front of their desks. It is counterproductive, however, to sit in the same spot for more than about forty-five or fifty minutes. The longer you sit in one spot, the more constricted your circulation becomes, and the more likely you are to get stiff and develop cramps in your back and neck. There's nothing more distracting than some physical discomfort if you're trying to concentrate on a difficult intellectual problem. So include in your schedule each day regular periods for getting up, stretching, and walking around to relax those cramped muscles. Get the blood flowing more freely to your brain again! Otherwise, you may find you're putting in plenty of time at your desk, but you're sinking regularly into a semicomatose state from lack of physical activity.

Learn to go with the flow. Finally, if your mind keeps wandering in the direction of other work you need to do, rather than the particular tasks you've set for yourself, it may be smart to plunge right into the subject that has control of your mind at the moment. For example, if you're working on a particular marketing problem and find your mind keeps drifting to a report your boss wants you to write, try changing your schedule. Drop the marketing report, and let your interest in the project for your boss carry you in that direction. You'll be doing your work in a slightly different order than you had planned, but you may find yourself working much more efficiently because of a natural interest in the subject matter.

I've devoted a fair amount of space to getting mean in the morning because I'm convinced that the key to a successful day is the progress you make in the first half hour in your office. If you start by putting things off, you'll find yourself falling into a pattern where you begin to procrastinate at other points during the day. And such a pattern is ready-made to give you a negative attitude not only toward that particular day, but also toward your job and yourself as well. You can succeed only if you feel good about yourself and your potential on the job, so it's essential to establish a positive feeling the first minute you walk into the office, or you'll find yourself facing an uphill, depressing climb for the rest of the day.

Sometimes, however, no matter how fast a start you get in the morning, you'll still be tempted later in the day to put certain things off, either because they bore you, or you find them so distasteful you don't even want to think about them. At this point, I'd like to go into a little more detail about how to overcome these other serious periods of procrastination.

CHAPTER 21

The Perils of Procrastination

Everybody puts things off at one time or another. We procrastinate in the prayerful hope that hard, unpleasant tasks will go away, and we won't have to worry about them anymore. Somehow, some things *do* vanish, and that encourages us to delay completing other things.

The problem is that some things don't go away, and the chronic procrastinator often fails to take constructive action that will enrich his life and carry him one step further toward his ultimate goal of success. If there is an important task that I know I'm likely to delay acting upon, I often rely on one or more of these "procrastination prods" to keep me moving toward my goal.

1. NAG YOURSELF ON PAPER. Suppose you think you should study French because many of your business deals involve French-speaking clients, but somehow you can't seem to get started on a course. You can nag yourself into action by jotting down, *Sign up for Berlitz course* at the top of your appointment diary each day.

If you find you're getting used to seeing that reminder on your memo pad, try writing it in several provocative ways. For example, you may feel that you have a better chance of moving up in your company if you get some background in accounting. So you may start off by writing down, *I've got to learn accounting.* If that doesn't work, and you find you're just transferring that note from one day to the next without caring about what it means, sit down and do some thinking. If you decide that extra education will mean a $20-a-week raise, write that down, *Learn accounting and earn $20 more each week (or $1040 more each year).* If that still doesn't work, try something else, *If I become an accountant, my wife will be proud of me.* Or, *My mother-in-law will like me.*

All this may strike you as a childish game, but after all, that's what most procrastination is: playing childish games with yourself to avoid extra work or responsibilities. The purpose of this memo pad exercise is not only to worry yourself into action, but also to help you think through all the implications of your failure to act.

2. PUT YOURSELF ON THE SPOT BY TELLING OTHERS ABOUT YOUR PLANS AND DEADLINES. It's much easier to put off things if you're the only person involved in the project. But if you have other people depending on you, their presence will exert a definite pressure on you to get moving and meet the deadlines you've set for yourself and them.

Bring your secretary into the initial stages of each of your projects by asking her to remind you that the deadline is arriving, or give her a specific assignment related to the beginning of the project. Then, if you fail to uphold your part of the project, you'll be wasting her time as well as your own.

If it's not possible to bring anyone else into the beginning of the project, at least brag to one or more people about what you plan to do so that they'll be likely to ask you about it, to see how you're coming along. When you're at church or a club meeting, for instance, tell a friend: "By this time next week, I'm going to be well under way on that new sales promotion campaign I was telling you about. I'll give you a blow-by-blow description the next time I see you."

It's also helpful to discuss your procrastination problem with your spouse or a close friend and ask him or her to prod you into action. One person I know even suggested the formation of a Procrastinators Anonymous group, so that those who suffer from this problem could get together with fellow strugglers and provide some group reinforcement to combat the tendency to postpone everything.

3. Pick the path of least resistance in starting a project. I sometimes put off embarking on a business deal because the initial stages appear distasteful. Perhaps there's a great deal of paperwork, or unexciting research and analysis, or I know I'll have to lay out a fair amount of money and won't have much fun doing it until the project really gets rolling.

The fallacy in this line of thinking is that there's *always* an enjoyable way to start things off. The problem is simply to discover that path of least resistance. One way I like to begin something is to make a luncheon date with a person who is doing something similar to what I'm about to attempt. It's relatively painless to lean back in a chair at a nice restaurant and discuss problems I'm likely to encounter and ways to overcome them. Perhaps you'd prefer to meet someone like this for a tennis date or a play. Whatever the excuse for the appointment, you're at least taking a step which is easing you in the most pleasant way toward your goal. The most important thing in overcoming procrastination is just getting started. Once you begin to move, your momentum will build, and you'll find your progress toward the completion of your project getting smoother and smoother.

4. BEFORE YOU START, BREAK DOWN EVERY JOB OR GOAL INTO ITS COMPONENT PARTS, AND THEN WORK ON EACH PART INDIVIDUALLY. One of the reasons that many people find themselves resisting a job is that they look at the *entire* task and decide it's too overwhelming to think about at the moment. But if they were to plan a way to move gradually through the work, one step at a time, it would seem less formidable, and there would be less inclination to procrastinate.

The best football coach, for example, always stresses playing one game at a time—even one play at a time. He knows if his players start to think about the headlines or the conference championship or Super Bowl, they'll fail to tend to the business at hand and may lose against an easy opponent.

Similarly, if you decide you want to save $600 additional dollars each year, you'll probably never get started toward your goal unless you break it down on a month-by-month basis. The New York-based *Church Business Report*, an executive newsletter for pastors and congregations, suggested a "mini-money" principle in a recent issue to achieve just such an objective. First, the letter said, you should think in terms of saving $50 a month instead of $600 a year. Then, break down the $50 a month into separate items of about $5 each. For example, if you and your spouse buy two newspapers each day, try getting along on one instead. At 20¢ a paper, that would amount to $5.20 a month for daily papers (excluding Sundays). The idea, in other words, is to find enough $5 items to bring your total up to $50 a month, and then continue this program for a year to save $600. It's much easier to embark on such a project if you can think initially in terms of saving $5 rather than $600.

Procrastination is an insidious personality flaw because there are so many valuable things in life that remain quietly in the background. They don't demand your attention or put pressure on you to start them, but at the same time they do offer great happiness and success if you just claim them for your own. I'll never forget the wonderful speech of the little girl in Thornton Wilder's *Our Town*, where she tells the mother to look at her closely—that she'll be a child for just a few years, and it will never be possible to live these times again. I get tears in my eyes every time I read that passage because I know some of the most marvelous things in life will be lost because of the tendency to postpone taking action on them. Satisfying, rewarding relationships with your loved ones are an essential backdrop for the ultimately satisfying career. Yet you're so quick to say, "I'll go camping with my son later," or "I'll spend time reading the Bible to Suzy next week." Of course, "later" and "next week" may never arrive, and months or years later you will inherit the guilt from that neglected relationship.

So that you won't leave this chapter still in a state of procrastination, I encourage you to stop reading this book for half an hour or even for the rest of the day, if necessary, and try this exercise. First, write down those things you've failed to do in both your business and personal life. Then, to the side of each item, indicate the first step you should take toward achieving those objectives. Finally, get started!

Now, if you've made some moves toward accomplishing each of these goals you've been putting off, it's time to consider one of the simplest of all time management techniques—the fine art of saying: No.

CHAPTER 22

The Fine Art of Saying No

The higher you rise in your field and the more expertise you acquire, the more you'll find that other people want to get you to do some work for them as well. Quickly there comes a point at which you no longer have any time left, and if you keep accepting new responsibilities, you'll soon find you're doing nothing well.

The simple solution to this problem is just to turn people down, but that's one of the most difficult things to do. There are countless reasons why you can't say no. For example, you don't like to reject friends and risk hurting their feelings. Or you're interested in many things and are afraid you may miss out on an exciting project if you give a negative reply. Or you're so insecure that you fear the person you've turned down will dislike you. But no matter how compelling the reason, there comes a point at which you have to restrict your activities if you hope to remain a happy, effective successful worker.

The first stage in learning to say no is to decide which offers you're going to turn down and which you're going to accept. To make this decision, I'd suggest you turn back to those chapters that deal with setting your goals in life and establishing priorities in your daily work schedule. In general, you should seriously consider doing those things which further your main goals in life, and be wary of offers, no matter how attractive, which are outside the mainstream of your career development. Of course, sometimes an extremely compelling possibility may present itself to you unexpectedly, and it may be well to consider reevaluating and perhaps changing your ultimate goals in light of this new opportunity. But in general, always try to be ruthless in turning down anything that will divert you from the major goals you've set for yourself.

One of the most difficult negative decisions for me occurred in 1968, just after Richard Nixon was elected to the presidency. We were longtime friends, and I still called him "Dick" in those days, just before he assumed office. He met me backstage at the Welcome Home party at the Anaheim Center and said, point blank: "Art, I'd like you to be Ambassador to Australia. It's an especially important job now because we're involved in the Vietnam War. Our relationships in that part of the world are more important than ever before. What do you think?"

I had traveled extensively in Australia, and as I've said, I owned property there, so I knew what Australia was like—a place I liked to visit but not one where I particularly wanted to live, especially in the capital, Canberra. But my geographical preferences weren't the main consideration. I don't like cocktail parties and the political rituals that go with such a post, and the idea of working for any organization, including the government, where I know I'm only a front and the real power lies in Washington doesn't appeal to me.

But I knew I couldn't just turn the President-elect of

the United States down flat, so I said: "Dick, which would you rather have me do: Go and be our representative in Australia, or attempt to save thousands of young people from the ravages of drug abuse in this country? I have lectures, films, books, and fund-raising activities scheduled for this next year. I believe I'm more effective outside the government, so why not just put me on a commission to fight drugs?"

He agreed. After all, how could the President of the United States say anything negative about efforts to fight the drug problem in this country? Being an ambassador didn't fit in with my goals, and no was the only answer I could give Richard Nixon. But the way I did it points up something important about the *method* of turning an offer down: It's not always necessary to give a direct negative answer. There are many ways of saying no without actually saying it. In this encounter with Nixon, I merely offered him another choice, which I knew he would accept.

Another way to turn somebody down is to memorize a standard answer like this: "Fred, there's nothing I'd like better than to do what you propose, but you know my rule: I don't do anything unless I can do it well. And I can't do that now because there are too many things on my schedule that need to be done first."

Here, you stress the other fellow's welfare and interests and explain at the same time how busy you are. Frankly, I much prefer a direct answer like this, even though it's couched in pleasant phrases, to the runaround some businessmen give you. The worst kind of indefinite answer—which nevertheless amounts to a no—is the typical response of the Hollywood producer, "Don't call us, we'll call you." Or the producer may say, "We'll be in touch," but you never hear from him again. Another way to keep someone hanging is to agree in a general way with the proposal but say, "We'll have to work out the details later—now is a bad time." A standard joke in the California building trade in recent years is that suppliers will agree to everything a builder wants just to end the conversation. They tell you, "Yeah, you'll have ten truckloads of cement over there next Monday," but you both know it won't be there. This is a terrible way to do business, and as far as I'm concerned, much worse in the long run for business relationships than a simple, "No, I can't help you right now."

One final note on this subject: If you have to say no, it's bound to be relatively unpleasant both for you and the other person, so follow that principle discussed previously. Give your negative answer early in the morning—or as soon as you can after you make your decision—so that it won't hang over your head and distract your attention from the rest of your work. If you're like most people, the longer you wait, the more likely you are to play the upcoming conversation over and over in your mind, and after a certain point, this amounts to wasted mental energy. Say your no quickly and pleasantly, but decisively—that's the essence of the art!

CHAPTER 23

The Punctuality Imperative

Punctuality is one of the major imperatives in the life of a successful businessperson. Being late can sometimes sink a business deal and will always annoy the person waiting on you.

Despite my other faults, I've never had a problem with punctuality—primarily because I've lived my whole life with a stopwatch ticking in my ear. Most of my work on radio and television was done live, and when that red light went on, you had to be sitting there because the cameras had already started rolling. If you were even ten seconds late, it was fatal for the production.

As a result of this conditioning, I get very impatient when other people are late for meetings with me because I regard them as selfish individuals who are stealing my time. Everyone is late from time to time, perhaps because of an unavoidable delay such as a traffic jam. But some people develop a pattern of chronic lateness, and that's the kind of personality quirk that I find particularly offensive.

Marilyn Monroe became a legendary figure in the annals of Hollywood lateness. She kept studios, stars and directors waiting for as long as six to eight hours before showing up. Some felt she used these delays as a weapon to compensate for her own insecurities. In other words, by the time she finally arrived, she had pushed her own personal anxieties over onto those who were waiting for her and tried to make them feel as uncertain and inadequate as she did.

The reasons that most other people are always late are probably considerably less complex than Marilyn's. But I think they're just as important to understand as an initial step in achieving a greater degree of punctuality. Generally speaking, most lateness is due to a lack of consideration for others, or a lack of personal organization, or a desire to get that last little thing done before leaving your previous tasks.

1. LACK OF CONSIDERATION FOR OTHERS. There's a famous lawyer in Beverly Hills who casually shows up at private dinner parties when everyone else is eating dessert. I've been there when ten people would be chatting over their parfaits, and this guy would barge in and say, "Hi, everybody! Good to be here! What do we have tonight?"

The maddening thing—especially for the host and hostess—is that he never makes any effort to give an excuse for his tardiness. If he could just say he ran over a little old lady or a bomber blew up his car, that would at least be an acknowledgment he knows he's in the wrong.

If you're guilty of this sort of thing, it may be that you've just been oblivious about what you've been doing, and this illustration will serve as a reminder. But if after reading this, you find you still don't care about what other people think, at least take some practical considerations into account: A significant number of people, myself included, get extremely annoyed by this sort of late behavior. So if you continue in your tardiness, you're likely to gain a bad reputation and certainly will put yourself at a disadvantage with those individuals who put a high value on punctuality.

2. LACK OF PERSONAL ORGANIZATION. A singing star I know—one of the sweetest, most thoughtful guys in many ways—is always late. He's another person who always smiles brightly when he arrives and never excuses himself. Unfortunately for him, he gives the impression he's not a very well-organized person, and that can discourage potential partners from considering him in a deal.

Many businessmen judge you in the first few moments you're in their presence. If you walk into their office late, perspiring, with hair disheveled and papers protruding from your briefcase, the total image is not going to be one that inspires a great deal of confidence. Most of the people who run the American business community value their time highly, so if you have a business appointment, be there right on the dot, or even a little ahead of time. For social engagements, on the other hand, it's often best to be a little late, though customs vary around the country. My wife, Lois, and I made the mistake in our early days in Hollywood of ringing the bell right at 7:30 if the hostess had told us 7:30. As a result, we could hear people hurrying around inside, trying to throw their clothes on and swearing never to invite the Linkletters again. In this society, 7:30 really means something like 7:45.

3. THE GET-ONE-MORE-THING-DONE SYNDROME. One of the most common reasons for tardiness is the inner compulsion some people have to spend a few extra minutes on the job at hand or to put the finishing touches on

something before they leave for their next appointment. I have this problem myself sometimes, especially if I'm really engrossed in a project. The only way I know to overcome this tendency is for you to decide ahead of time when you need to leave to make it to your next engagement on time. Then, be ruthless in quitting your present task at least fifteen minutes ahead of time (more than fifteen minutes if you need time to dress or make other involved preparations for your departure).

One couple I know always have difficulty cutting off one task and moving on to the next, and their lateness can infuriate me if I'm the one waiting for them. We used to go skiing together, but they were always getting involved in telephone calls or conversations that made them late, and I'd be fuming at the bottom of the hill with all my skiing equipment weighing me down. For an avid skier, there's nothing worse than to have all your gear on, to be slightly ahead of the crowd, and then to see the slopes getting more and more packed with people as you wait for your tardy companions. That sort of experience ruins the entire morning for me: I would get so mad I could hardly speak civilly to them, and I finally decided that if we hoped to maintain any kind of relationship, we shouldn't plan to ski together.

Understanding all the possible reasons that can make you late will help you to overcome the problem, but punctuality, more than anything else, is basically a matter of becoming sensitive to the feelings of other people. If you put yourself in the other guy's place and imagine how you would feel—either in a business or social setting—if he were late, you may find you're more inclined to do something about your lack of punctuality. Some people fall back on gimmicks like setting their watches ahead so that they can be late according to the watch but punctual according to the real time. If that works for you, there's nothing wrong with it. But for most people, tardiness is a more basic problem that involves becoming more considerate of other human beings, rather than falling back on superficial tricks and techniques.

Finally, punctuality includes not only getting to an appointment on time but also leaving before you've overstayed your welcome. I know people who come to our home for dinner and stand around in the vestibule for a half hour talking. They simply will not leave until Lois or I sigh, look at our watches, or make some other movement to indicate the evening is finished. The same thing happens to me, sometimes, with business appointments. A salesman may get to my office five minutes early, but then he keeps talking and repeating himself and emphasizing his points until I'm ready to throw him out. Even if you've laid the groundwork for a good sale, if you have to be pushed out of the office, the last thing your prospective buyer will remember is that emotion of irritability he experienced. That sour taste will not bode well for your next visit when you hope to close the deal.

This emphasis on the needs of people and the importance of putting yourself in the other guy's shoes leads me into the next and final section—the most important part of this book. In the last analysis, no matter how many techniques and practical approaches to success that you learn, you're heading for failure and unhappiness if you've failed to straighten out your personal value system. My own business experience has convinced me that feeling right about yourself inwardly—having a solid sense of spiritual stability—is the essential element, the *sine qua non* of success.

PART SIX

Spiritual Stability:
The <u>Sine Qua Non</u> of Success

CHAPTER 24

The Family Factor

One of the most important foundations for success is a secure, happy family life. These days, some people argue that broken marriages are such an everyday occurrence that they shouldn't have any impact on a person's career development. But in fact, divorce is a failure as devastating as any business debacle. The individual who fails to work hard to maintain his marriage and other family relationships is sowing the seeds of personal disorder and ineffectiveness. After all, how much time can a businessperson spend on creative thinking about the job when he's preoccupied with divorce or separation proceedings?

The first step in strengthening this major foundation of your life is to recognize how important your family is to you. This is no easy task because it means moving upstream, against the current of prevailing American practice and attitudes. I suffered a significant business failure a few years ago because I didn't understand how hard it is to make the strengthening of family values a priority in the average household. A religious business-man approached me about producing and selling a home study course to teach families how they could become closer and more loving and communicative. He told me that if I could get some other stars to endorse the course, we might become as successful as other home correspondence courses, and it would also do a great deal to help rebuild American family life.

The idea sounded great to me, so I contacted Pat Boone, Danny Thomas, the current Miss America, and a number of other well-known personalities. We got Dr. James Peterson, head of the Family Institute of the University of Southern California, among others, to put together a record album and other study material, which we decided to sell for about $100 a package.

But as interesting and useful as the whole thing looked on paper, the entire venture went down the drain. Potential customers agreed they needed such a course, but not enough people were willing to pay for it, and among those who did take it home, most put it on a shelf without working at it. This experience and others like it have convinced me that it takes more than a passing interest or sales promotion to make someone take his family seriously. What's needed is a deep commitment to make family life work, and this commitment has to be just as serious and heartfelt as any ambitions to make money or gain status in the business community.

There are two things that tend to undermine marriages in business societies: the growing public rejection of traditional sexual standards and excess consumption of liquor. Correcting these deficiencies could cut the divorce rate by 50 percent.

In America, today, there are countless "attractive nuisances," or sexually interesting and available young men and women who think there's nothing wrong with striking up an open sexual liaison with somebody else's spouse. Television, movies, and magazines like *Playboy* all wink at the old-fashioned Puritan standards, but the history of mankind argues differently. Remember this and you'll be less likely to fall into the trap of destroying your own family life and consequently getting into extracurricular activities that are certain to undercut your effectiveness at work.

I wouldn't hold myself up as some moral paragon, but I have always advocated rather traditional standards of sexual morality, and I've always put marriage very high on the scale of institutions that should be preserved and protected. As a result, I've developed a reputation as a family man, and those who comment on the Hollywood scene—and are constantly on the lookout for the self-righteous hypocrite—aren't about to let me forget it.

Columnist Hedda Hopper, for many years a close friend of ours, once told me: "Art, in all my years in Hollywood, I've lived through one disillusionment after another. People I've believed in have turned out to have feet of clay. Marriages I've lauded to the skies have exploded in my face. The most unlikely people have been unfaithful to their wives. I just hope I never find out anything about you."

Sighing, I replied, "I do too, Hedda."

"What do you mean by that?" she asked accusingly. Although I had intended no double meaning, her suspicious mind was already trying to read between the lines.

"Nothing, Hedda," I said.

"There better not be!" she snapped. And I knew if there were something going on, she and the other Hollywood pundits would be after me, even more eagerly than most other people, because I openly espoused traditional family values.

The more I developed a reputation through articles in family magazines, the more important it was for me to protect that reputation because, increasingly, I had a great deal to lose. Not only would I irreparably damage the great relationship I have with Lois, but my public would look at me in a different, less favorable light.

The same is true of you in a different way. Consider your relationship with your spouse. Apart from any moral or religious assumptions you may make—and I don't mean to downplay these values because I give them a high priority in my own life—just think for a moment about what you stand to lose for a little bit of ephemeral pleasure. Of course, that pleasure may seem all important at the moment it presents itself. In the film industry, actors and actresses run in and out of each other's dressing rooms and spend long hours together on location. It's inevitable that sexual encounters will become a factor in their relationships.

But what many people fail to realize is that what motivates a young woman to get involved may have more to do with career advancement or the desire for an influential husband than the man's raw animal magnetism. The "audition couch" is a well-known institution in Hollywood, and I know the same factors are at work in the business community between employees and their superiors. It's not always so easy, however, to protect yourself from the repercussions of that couch. Someone is bound to talk, and one furtive telephone call to your spouse can give you endless hours of worry and arguments at home and may eventually lead to the break-up of your marriage. Is this pain and uncertainty and distraction from your career objectives worth the indiscretion? I believe not, but that's something only you can decide.

To help you focus on just how much you have to be thankful for with your spouse, try the following exercise on a piece of paper. Answering these questions should give you an overview of your marital relationship and suggest a few steps you can take to improve it.

1. How many years have you been married?

2. When was the last time you complimented your spouse? State the nature of the compliment.

3. When did you and your spouse have your last fight? Indicate the subject of your disagreement.

4. What issues do you fight about most often?

5. Indicate what you think you can do to prevent such fights in the future.

6. List what you consider the good points and strengths in your marriage.

7. List the three biggest problems you and your spouse face, and beside each problem, suggest ways you can solve it.

As you reflect on the problems you and your spouse face, remember that the principles I've discussed about success in life—including good conversation techniques and listening to the needs of the other person—often apply to family as well as business situations. I'm amazed, for example, at the number of husbands and wives who have forgotten how to talk to one another about the things in life that really matter. They can discuss which bills need to be paid or who should be invited over for the next dinner party. But they seem incapable of intimate discussions about what life means to them, about their deepest fears and anxieties, about their most intimate dreams for the future.

If this is one of your concerns, try a technique that worked for one young couple I know. The husband had fallen into the habit of watching television during the evening meal, and he would continue to stay glued to the screen as they sat around drinking their tea or coffee. As a result, this couple found that they did very little meaningful communicating after they came home from work at night. The solution to their difficulty came when the wife suggested: "Why don't we start going out to dinner more often? It costs more money but would be cheaper and less expensive than marriage therapy!" So they began to eat at inexpensive restaurants several nights a week, and they discovered one another again. It's almost impossible during an hour's meal, when you're looking at the other person with nothing to distract you, not to get into those deep conversations that should involve every married couple.

Many of you undoubtedly listed alcohol as one of your major problems, and I know there's no easy solution to this one. Of all the drugs I know about, this one is by far the worst. Excessive drinking is the cause of more marital discord and career problems than any other single thing I know. I don't know how often I've seen a person get drunk at an office party and tell an immediate superior what he really thinks of him, or make an embarrassing move with the young woman he's been ogling secretly for months.

If you haven't developed a serious problem yet, I'd just encourage you to take some time before each party you attend and consider the consequences of excessive drinking. Ask yourself if it's really worth it—alienating a boss or a valuable social contact by getting sloppily and obnoxiously inebriated. Drinking excessively at home also impairs your ability to communicate with your spouse, so it's important to consider whether temporary dulling of the senses and lightheadedness justify damaging and per-haps destroying your marriage.

If your spouse's drinking problem has already gone so far that it borders on alcoholism, counseling with your pastor or a psychotherapist, or getting him or her inter-ested in an organization like Alcoholics Anonymous may be the only solution. But whatever you decide, start work-ing toward that end right now, for the future of your marriage probably hangs in the balance.

Building a stable, secure family life must begin with your spouse, but it can't end there. No matter how se-cure and loving the relationship between husband and wife, there will always be unhappiness, discontent, and time- and energy-wasting anxiety if you've failed to tend to the welfare of your children.

I've spent a lot of time interviewing and studying kids. In a way, I consider them to be my specialty. My experi-ence with youngsters has convinced me that there are three key factors that go into any successful parent-child relationship, and these can be summed up by the acronym RAP, or responsibility, authority, and participation.

When I say responsibility, I'm not just referring to the sense of responsibility parents should have for their chil-dren—though that certainly is very important. Just as significant is the responsibility that the parent should inculcate into the child. I've been asked after lectures whether or not I think kids should have to work for their spending money, and my answer is always an unequivocal Yes! The pain and sweat and agony that many older people had to go through to earn a living in the 1930s and '40s may have been unpleasant, to say the least. But the trials and difficulties they learned to overcome gave them muscles—and I don't mean just the physical kind.

They got tough and resilient inside, ready for any disaster or problem. They knew they could earn a living with their hands if the white-collar jobs ran out, because they had done it as youngsters. I'm often reminded of the financial vice-president of several companies in the South and Southwest who had just lost his job. He told his son: "I know I'll have a job in another month or two, even if it's pumping gas at the local station. I did that years ago, and I can do it again. I'm not too proud to do any kind of work for my family."

That's the kind of inner moral fiber that I'm afraid too many young people have lost, but I'd like to see them recapture it again. And the only way they'll be able to recapture it is through the training and values that the parents in this country pass on to their children.

As for authority—the next letter in RAP—that doesn't mean authoritarianism or a dictatorial attitude that demands unreasoning compliance with orders. Kids simply won't obey that kind of control, or if they do for a while, they'll eventually rebel completely against it. Rules firmly and lovingly applied are essential to the development of any healthy child. Kids may scream about a 10 P.M. or 11 P.M. curfew, but if they're always dealt with in a consistent and disciplined manner, they'll be reasonable. They may even come to understand that the reason for tougher rules than some of their friends have is that their parents are especially concerned about their welfare.

Finally, participation with your children in a variety of activities is absolutely essential if you hope to get your value system across to them in a way that will influence their lives. On one level, this involves relating to them as human beings—not keeping yourself on some pedestal where they feel reluctant to confide their own troubles to you. The reason there are so many hotlines for kids with venereal disease, drug problems, and runaway tendencies is that there are no parents at home who have offered a sympathetic ear.

It's also necessary to schedule enjoyable, trouble-free dinners even more often—say at least four or five times a week. Even on those evenings when we had dinner parties to attend, we would still sit down with the kids around the family table for a salad or piece of fruit before we left. These times together gave us a chance to teach them good manners and also to listen to their current thinking and problems.

To get them talking, you might say: "I just read they threw some boys out of Annapolis for cheating. What do you think about that? Do you see much of that at school?"

One of the kids might reply, "Yeah, everybody's cheating."

"You don't say. Well, how do you feel about that? Do you think you'd ever like to cheat?"

"Yeah, once in a while I cheat."

Then you might launch into a discussion of why people cheat and discuss the morality of the problem, but never to condemn them or make them feel you don't accept them. How you feel about cheating would become apparent but not with an authoritarian, judgmental, "Thou-shalt-not cheat" attitude, which would probably encourage them to cheat even more.

We always tried to avoid angry arguments or disciplinary judgments because we didn't want the kids' memories of our meals together to be tinged with indigestion. But good humor and laughter were always in order. One of the things that used to give us the biggest chuckle was a joke I'd pull on the baby of the family. By age two, the youngest would always sit to my left in a high chair, and I would make him feel important by pushing on his nose to call our kitchen helper to the table. Of course the buzzer was actually near my chair under the table, but the child never knew that until he got old enough to move to another chair and make way for the next younger sister or brother. He thought his nose was magic!

Bringing up children properly and getting along with your spouse are uncertain ventures at best, no matter how hard you try. I know that from personal experience because I went through periods of self-recrimination after the death of our daughter, Diane, wondering where I'd gone wrong. But I'm convinced that stressing these three key elements—responsibility, authority, and participation—will put you in as good a position as possible to provide a secure family base from which to pursue success in life. As for those unexpected tragedies and difficulties that no prior preparations can overcome, it's sometimes necessary to draw on even deeper personal resources to find the strength to bounce back and move on to greater levels of achievement.

CHAPTER 25

Your Inner Life

In the early pages of this book, I said I believe success is a journey, not a destination. If the rewards of success become ends in themselves, then the focus is primarily on money, status, and power, and the greatest pinnacles of happiness will probably always be elusive. Paradoxically, the fruits of success often come most easily to those who stress other values in life. Successful people can find true happiness only if their high level of achievement is accompanied by deep-rooted character traits that enhance their relationships with family, friends, and God.

I've been particularly impressed by how inadequate money is as an ultimate goal of a successful life. Unfortunately, money is a scorecard of success. I know people with $50 million in a certain neighborhood who will hardly deign to associate with those with $20 million living in a less important section. This sort of attitude strikes me as not only silly; it's self-destructive as well. Those who are constantly consumed with accumulating more and more completely lose sight of those things that really count in life. One man I know, who has reached a logical extreme with this attitude, once told me: "When I die and the amount of money I have is printed in the newspapers, it will absolutely crush some of my friends! They have no idea how much more I own than they do!"

I've seen this kind of self-consuming avarice actually hold people back from achieving truly great things because their vision of life is too narrow. They gradually lose their ability to enjoy life.

Your real destination should not be just success in business with the money and power that go along with it, but developing good character traits that make you a better person and more complete human being. Although it would be easy to list dozens of valuable personal traits, I've discovered four that are the most significant among the happy and successful people I know: humility, patience, courage, and spirituality.

1. HUMILITY. This may not be the first quality you would associate with a hard-driving, successful business leader, but in fact, it can be one of the main things that endears you to clients and colleagues and makes them want to work with you. On the other hand, if you're an obviously self-centered person, you're going to alienate many more people than you influence. One Hollywood actor bored a companion to tears one evening by talking for more than an hour about himself. Then, as if aware that he had gone too far, he said: "Look, we've been talking only about me. Now, let's talk about *you*. What do *you* think of my latest picture?"

There is a fine line between self-promotion, which can still leave room for genuine humility, and blatant self-aggrandizement, which is sure to antagonize fellow workers. Part of the secret of staying on the side of acceptable self-promotion is to admit your faults or mistakes, as well as display your strengths. Developing a personality that combines openness and vulnerability with aggressiveness can help give you a human quality that goes a long way in the business world.

2. PATIENCE. This is a virtue I had to learn early in my career during an excruciating experience which was to have a lasting impact on my future. As co-owner with John Guedel of the fledgling "People Are Funny" radio show, I ran into a personality problem with a well-known entertainer named Art Baker who co-starred with me on the program. After the fourth show, Baker abruptly said that he didn't think we were working out as a team, and that one of us would have to go. I told him I was sorry he felt that way, and I'd discuss it with my partner, Guedel.

Guedel and I both agreed that although Baker's name was an asset—he was far better known nationally than I was at the time—there was nothing we could do if he wanted out. Besides, we were both certain that I could carry the program without him if we brought in a staff announcer to handle the introductions and some commercials.

John called our Chicago sponsors to inform them of the change and reassure them the program would go smoothly, but the sponsors didn't see things quite that way. Their advertising agency said: "If Art Linkletter and Art Baker can't work together, the better known Art will stay, and the other one will have to go. Otherwise, I don't think we can continue the program."

I was shattered. Here I was with my first coast-to-coast show of which I was one of the co-owners, and I was being asked to leave! I realize now that most ad agency people can get extremely rattled if they think a key element in a new show may be removed. And I learned later that Art Baker had contacted them before he ever sat down to talk with me and had convinced them he was the mainstay of the show.

John Guedel was completely loyal to me. "That does it!" he said. "We'll take the show off the air!" But I knew he had put all his financial resources into "People Are Funny," and I still had some radio work I was doing in San Francisco, so for the good of the show, I decided to go. That meant heading back to San Francisco. For one entire year I stayed there, doing local programs and writing stunt ideas and material for "People Are Funny" —jokes and routines that Art Baker used on the air.

That was the most galling twelve months in my professional life. But finally, when the show had been established on its own merits, I returned to Hollywood, John Guedel replaced Art Baker with me, and the rest is broadcasting history. My year of "exile" in San Francisco taught me, more than anything else, how important it is to be patient and tough in struggling toward the goals you set for yourself in life. It was frustrating and nerve-racking to sit up there and feed material to a show I realized might never have me as a star. I knew John Guedel was absolutely trustworthy, but I was also aware of the tremendous pressures that could move the program in a direction we hadn't planned. There was constant temptation just to forget the whole thing and concentrate exclusively on my work in San Francisco. But I wanted a national program, so I stuck it out and eventually prevailed. Patience and the endurance to stick out a tough situation are, indeed, often the pivotal qualities that lead a person to success or failure in business.

3. COURAGE. If you have achieved a high degree of success, you have taken chances with your future at one time or another. You would never have gotten anywhere if you

had been afraid to venture forth and put your experience and financial resources on the line. What I'm talking about is not some sort of foolhardy risk-taking, but a willingness to act with realistic courage on your convictions. Walt Disney was the kind of man who had this strong inner fiber of courage, and this strength of his was never revealed more clearly than when he invited me out to evaluate one of his planned business ventures in the early 1950s.

We were very good friends, and Lois and I spent a great deal of our leisure time with Walt and his wife, Lillian. The Disney Studio in Burbank was doing very well in those days, and he had every reason to be happy and satisfied. But being the creative, venturesome person that he was, he was getting restless. He asked me to take a ride with him out into the country, and we must have driven for about twenty-five miles through orange groves and fields in Orange County. Then we turned off the main road, near Anaheim, and drove along some groves until we reached a large expanse of land, uninhabited except for a few grazing horses and some abandoned sheds.

After we got out of the car and started walking over the land, the place was transformed in my mind's eye as Walt described his vision. He talked about places called "Tomorrowland" and "Fantasyland," and described where they would be situated in a huge entertainment complex called "Disneyland," which would be built right on the ground where we were standing. It wasn't imaginary to Walt. He was actually seeing it as well as the millions of people from all over the world who he believed would come here to enjoy it.

But I began to grow more and more concerned. Who

in the world, I thought, is going to drive twenty-five miles to ride a roller coaster? Not only that, the bare logistics of the thing staggered me. Walt Disney was proposing to create a city dedicated to relaxation and amusement with all the financial and construction problems that starting such a project from scratch implied.

I had such admiration for his business acumen and his show-business savvy that I hardly knew how to tell him I thought he was making the biggest, most ruinous mistake of his entire life. Then he got to the reason for bringing me to his undeveloped land:

"Art," he said, "financially I can handle only Disneyland itself. It will take everything I have as it is. But the land bordering it, where we're standing now, will be jammed with hotels and motels and restaurants and convention halls to accommodate the people who will come to spend their entire vacations here at my park in just a couple of years. I've bought all I can afford. And I want you," Walt continued, "to have an opportunity to get some of the surrounding acreage because it will increase in value several hundred times in the next five years."

What could I say? I *knew* he was wrong. I knew that he had let a dream get the best of his common sense, so I mumbled something about a tight-money situation and promised that I would look into the whole thing a little later on.

"Later will be too late," he cautioned me as we walked back to the car. "You had better move on it right now."

I remember our short walk along that dry, sandy road very vividly because that little stroll probably cost me about a million dollars a step. But my hesitancy—and undoubtedly the skepticism of many of his close associates—didn't sway Walt from his purpose. He had not only the capacity to envision the project, but also the guts to carry it out, and this is where that extraordinary inner fiber of courage took over. Soaring construction costs and unpredictable disasters began to tax his capital severely. Once, for example, an entire shipment of bathroom fixtures arrived too damaged to be used and had to be replaced. He had some insurance for this loss, but by the time the litigation between the manufacturer and shipper had been straightened out, Disneyland was already in full operation. Walt had to come up with extra cash for those fixtures at the time they were damaged.

Financial difficulties struck him again and again, so that when Disneyland was finally ready for the first press preview, Walt was down to his last resources. That, to me, represents the essence of courage, and his courage paid off in financial dividends for him, jobs for thousands, and pleasure for millions from around the world. He had been right, of course, about that land he suggested that I buy. The place is covered with hotels, motels, restaurants, and convention halls, and as he had predicted, millions do go there to spend their vacations. I don't think he foresaw that a 55,000-seat baseball park would be built across the road to house the California Angels, but knowing how closely Walt's imagination paralleled future reality, I wouldn't be surprised.

4. SPIRITUALITY. The most effective way of tying these traits of humility, patience, and courage together seems to be with the spiritual cement of faith in God. I'm not saying, of course, that it's necessary to believe in God to achieve the money, power, and prestige that are usually associated with worldly achievement. But I do believe that a kind of stillness and confidence at the center of

your spiritual being is necessary if you hope to *enjoy* your success to the fullest.

It's not as though I've been interested in spiritual things all my life, either. I was brought up in a Christian home with a father—an evangelical preacher—who was regarded by some as a borderline fanatic, so zealous was he in his convictions. Dad Linkletter's table grace was a mini-sermon, a detailed "Thank you" to the Almighty that cited chapter and verse to substantiate our appreciation of His bounty. Years later, I like to tell audiences that grace took so long at our table that I was sixteen before a hot meal crossed my lips. While perhaps a slight exaggeration, the illustration does suggest the intense religious atmosphere that prevailed during my youth.

I reacted adversely to this early childhood environment after I left home to attend college, and I didn't move back in God's direction until Diane's death. During most of my career, I found it difficult to acknowledge or believe that anyone but myself was responsible for plotting my journey through life. But when my daughter took her life, I found myself floundering, angry, and confused. The old moorings that had made life so certain and my success so secure no longer seemed adequate.

I'll never forget that first terrible night of her death after flying back from Colorado Springs. As Lois, Dawn, my eldest daughter, and I walked across the reception area of the Los Angeles International airport, people came up with tears in their eyes to grab my hand impulsively and say they were sorry. These weren't autograph seekers. They were simply people who wanted us to know they really cared.

I remember thinking, as I rubbed the moisture from my own eyes, that I knew for the first time what "I'm sorry" really means. I've never used those words since then to someone else without a special personal commitment that is missing so often in ritual expressions of sympathy. In some respects, the cold, commercial atmosphere of a busy metropolitan airport is a strange place to witness God's compassion through the eyes and words of fellow Christians. But I felt His presence that day shielding my wife, my daughter, and myself as we rushed toward a waiting car. "It's all right, Art," someone seemed to tell me. "This is one you won't have to fight by yourself."

God's plan for my life has become more evident in the years since that experience, and my growing faith has enabled me to relax in the success I've achieved. True success, as far as I'm concerned, is the ability to take the money, status, and other achievements in stride, as bench-marks along life's journey and not as ends in themselves. For it's only by discovering some ultimate purpose behind it all that compulsive strivings after worldly triumphs can be transformed into a truly satisfying and meaningful way of life.

About the Author

Art Linkletter is preeminently qualified to write about success in business and life for he has enjoyed international acclaim as a radio and television performer, a best-selling author, an astute businessman, and a popular lecturer.

His long-running radio and television shows, "People Are Funny," and "House Party," established him as a highly successful on-the-air salesman and brought enjoyment to millions for more than three decades. His book *Kids Say the Darndest Things* still ranks as one of the most popular books ever published in the United States. Shifting his attention gradually from the entertainment to the business world in the 1950s and 1960s, Mr. Linkletter founded Linkletter Enterprises, Inc., a conglomerate which has specialized in oil exploration, construction, Australian cattle ranching, and other ventures. More recently, he has focused his energies on lecturing about success to thousands at conventions and positive-thinking rallies in this country and abroad. He has also served on the boards of directors of ten national corporations, including MGM, Diners Club, and National Liberty Insurance Company.

Finally, Mr. Linkletter has spent a considerable amount of time in the last few years working for non-profit causes, particularly in the area of drug abuse prevention. He has addressed the General Assembly of the United Nations on the subject of drugs, has been President of the National Coordinating Council on Drug Abuse Education and Information, and has also served on the President's Advisory Council on Drug Abuse. His other commitments have included being a member of the President's commission to improve reading in the United States; the United States member for UNESCO; a roving ambassador-at-large for the United States Commerce Department; and a member of the boards of trustees of Springfield College in Massachusetts and the Art Center College of Design in Los Angeles. Mr. Linkletter has also been awarded ten honorary doctorates from various colleges and universities.